Madrid

by Paul Wade and Kathy Arnold

Freelance journalists Kathy Arnold and
Paul Wade have been regular visitors to Spain
for many years. They have written and edited
25 books, including AA publications such as
On The Road New England, and Thomas Cook
guides to London, Normandy and the Loire
Valley. They contribute to American magazines,
UK national newspapers, radio and
television programmes.

Above: *Plaza Mayor*

AA Publishing

Take your binoculars to appreciate the ceiling at El Escorial's library

Written by Paul Wade and Kathy Arnold.
Updated by Christopher and Melanie Rice.
Original photography by Michelle Chaplow.

Published by AA Publishing, a trading name of Automobile Association Developments Limited, whose registered office is Southwood East, Apollo Rise, Farnborough, Hampshire, GU14 0JW. Registered number 1878835.

© Automobile Association Developments Limited 2000, 2005
Reprinted Aug 2001. Reprinted Apr 2002
Reprinted 2003. Information verified and updated.
This edition 2005. Information verified and updated.

A CIP catalogue record for this book is available from the British Library.

Find out more about AA Publishing and the wide range of travel publications and services the AA provides by visiting our website at www.theAA.com/bookshop

A01990

Colour separation: Keenes, Andover
Printed and bound in Italy by Printer Trento s.r.l.

Contents

About this Book 4

About this Book

This book is divided into five sections to cover the most important aspects of your visit to Madrid.

Viewing Madrid pages 5–14
An introduction to Madrid by the authors.
Madrid's Features
Essence of Madrid
The Shaping of Madrid
Peace and Quiet
Madrid's Famous

Top Ten pages 15–26
The authors' choice of the Top Ten places to see in Madrid, listed in alphabetical order, each with practical information.

What to See pages 27–90
The five main areas of Madrid, each with its own brief introduction and an alphabetical listing of the main attractions.
Practical information
Snippets of 'Did you know…' information
5 suggested walks
3 suggested drives
2 features

Where To… pages 91–116
Detailed listings of the best places to eat, stay, shop, take the children and be entertained.

Practical Matters pages 117–24
A highly visual section containing essential travel information.

Maps
All map references are to the individual maps found in the What to See section of this guide.
For example, El Prado has the reference 🗺️ 41E2 – indicating the page on which the map is located and the grid square in which the museum is to be found. A list of the maps that have been used in this travel guide can be found in the index.

Prices
Where appropriate, an indication of the cost of an establishment is given by € signs:
€€€ denotes higher prices, €€ denotes average prices, while € denotes lower charges.

Star Ratings
Most of the places described in this book have been given a separate rating:

😀😀😀   Do not miss
😀😀   Highly recommended
😀   Worth seeing

Viewing
Madrid

Above: *the centre of Spain is marked by Kilometre 0 in Puerta del Sol*
Right: *statue commemorating bullfighting legend Antonio Bienvenida outside Las Ventas bullring*

Paul Wade & Kathy Arnold's Madrid

Orienting Yourself
The heart of Madrid is compact. The *paseos* (boulevards), which run north–south, are the spine of the city. To the east is the vast Parque del Retiro (Retiro Park); to the west is the old quarter. Most of the attractions are within the square bordered by the Gran Vía (north side), the Palacio Real (west side) and the Rondas around the south.

Above: *bullfighting poster*
Right: *hand-painted directions to the Calle Mayor*
Below: *Plaza San Andrés*

Madrid was the capital of the world's first inter-continental empire. Between the 16th and 19th centuries, Spain ruled South, Central and much of North America, with colonies as far afield as the Philippines. No wonder every church seems more ornate than the last, and museums abound, crammed with masterpieces. The palaces are grand, ministries forbidding and houses enormous. When it comes to sheer grandeur, Madrid stands shoulder to shoulder with London, Paris and Rome.

The city has many faces. We enjoy exploring the medieval clutter of streets that scuttle away from the Plaza Mayor, down to the rabbit warren of La Latina and Lavapiés. Then there is the Habsburg quarter, west of the Puerta del Sol, and the high-class, trendy area of the *paseos* (boulevards) and Calle de Serrano. Walking around the city is a pleasure, but you can also hop on the Metro, the cheap, efficient and easy-to-use underground system linking every spot you will ever want to visit.

But most of all, this is a great place to have fun. *Madrileños* eat out constantly: you're never far from a coffee, a *caña* of beer or a glass of wine. Snacks abound, from sweet *churros* to salty *tapas*, served in bars walled with colourful tiles, and hung with faded photos of forgotten bullfighters. In summer, the *terrazas* (outdoor cafés) stay open until the early hours, causing traffic jams at three in the morning. All you need to get the best out of the city is stamina.

Madrid's Features

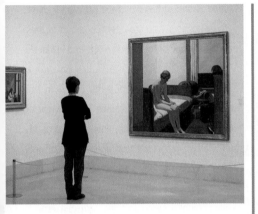

Geography

Madrid, the capital of Spain, is in the centre of the Iberian peninsula. Standing on a plateau some 650m above sea level, it is about 550–600km from both the Atlantic Ocean and the Mediterranean.

Climate

A Spanish saying describes Madrid as having nine months of winter and three months of hell. Certainly, winters are cold, with occasional snow, while summers are hot, with temperatures often over 35°C. Overall, the air is dry, with an annual average of 2,730 hours of sunshine. Spring and autumn are the best times of year to visit, with warm days and cool nights.

People and Economy

Over five million live in the province of Madrid, with three million in the city itself. Many come from other parts of Spain, as well as former Spanish colonies such as Argentina and Mexico.

Leisure Facilities

Madrid has at least 30 significant museums. Many are undergoing a much-needed upgrading to improve presentation and enjoyment by non-Spanish-speaking visitors. Few cities can rival the three jewels in Madrid's crown: the Museo del Prado (the Prado), the Museo Nacional Centro de Arte Reina Sofía and the Museo Thyssen-Bornemisza. In addition to cultural centres there are also amusement parks, swimming pools, a zoo and over 3,000 restaurants.

Province of Madrid
The metropolis is also the chief city of the province of Madrid, which encompasses 8,000sq km and includes cities such as Alcalá de Henares and Aranjuez. Just 52km to the north, the Sierra de Guadarrama provides skiing in the winter. Government and banking provide jobs in the city, and there are textile, food and metal-working industries in the surrounding area.

Above left: *contemplating Edward Hopper at Museo Thyssen-Bornemisza*
Above: *18th-century baroque entrance to the Museo Municipal*

Essence of Madrid

Madrid is one of the world's great capital cities, with inhabitants who are intensely proud of their traditions. They order *cocido madrileño* (a classic Madrid stew), stroll in the Retiro Park on a Sunday morning and dance the *chotis* in the street during the festival of San Isidro. Most of all they love to stay up late, eating dinner at 11, and chatting in the *terrazas* (open-air cafés) until dawn. While the days are devoted to boring essentials such as working, Madrid really comes to life at night – if you can't beat 'em, join 'em.

People-watching on the Plaza Mayor

THE **10** ESSENTIALS

If you only have a short time to visit Madrid, here are ten essentials, which together create a portrait of the city:

• **Buy the special *Abono Paseo del Arte* ticket and visit all three great art galleries**: the Prado (➤ 26), the Museo Nacional Centro de Arte Reina Sofía (➤ 19) and the Museo Thyssen-Bornemisza (➤ 22).

• **Tour the Palacio Real**, the monumental royal palace (➤ 23).

• **Drink a *fino* sherry** at La Venencia (➤ 97) or a vermouth with soda at Casa Alberto (➤ 96).

• **Order a *cocido madrileño*** (a classic Madrid stew), cooked in an earthenware pot by the fire at La Posada de la Villa (➤ 95).

• **Sip hot chocolate** and eat *churros* (like doughnuts) at the Chocolatería San Ginés (➤ 99).

• **Do what *madrileños* do on Sunday morning**: wander among the stamp and coin stalls on the Plaza Mayor (➤ 25); search for a bargain in the Rastro flea market (➤ 65); or stroll through the Retiro Park (➤ 24).

• **Go and watch a football** match at Real Madrid's Bernabéu Stadium (➤ 44), or at the Vicente Calderón stadium, home of rival Atlético Madrid.

• **Go shopping**, or window shopping, on Calle de Serrano (➤ 34) to see how the other half spends its money.

• **Take a siesta**; it's probably the only way you can stay up late.

• **Sit out at a *terraza*** (an open-air café), along the Paseo de la Castellana until two in the morning.

The Rastro market is a Sunday tradition

Souvenir-hunting on the Plaza Mayor

The Shaping of Madrid

Felipe II made Madrid his capital in 1561

Late 9th century
Muhammad I founds a Moorish village outpost called Magerit, 'the place of many springs'.

1083
Alfonso VI, King of Castile and Léon, captures Madrid, and gives the locals their nickname of *gatos* (cats) because of the numerous cats in the town.

1172
Death of Isidro Merlo y Quintana, aged 90. Later San Isidro Labrador, the labourer, is made patron saint of Madrid. His feast day is 15 May.

1309
Preparing to attack Granada, Fernando IV summons the parliament, the Cortes of Castile, to meet in Madrid for the first time.

1465
King Enrique IV awards Madrid the title of *muy noble y muy leal* (most noble and loyal). The city has some 20,000 inhabitants.

1477
Having united the kingdoms of Aragón and Castile by their marriage, Fernando and Isabel visit Madrid.

1544
Carlos I calls Madrid *imperial y coronada* (imperial and crowned).

1556
The first printing press is set up in Madrid.

1561
Felipe II moves his court to Madrid, the geographical centre of the country and now the capital of a vast empire.

1600
Felipe III is the first Spanish king born in Madrid.

1605
The first edition of Cervantes' classic story, *El Quijote* (*Don Quixote*), is published.

1613
The first town fire service is set up in Madrid.

1621
Under Felipe IV the arts flourish with names such as artist Diego de Velázquez and playwrights Lope de Vega, Calderón de la Barca and Tirso de Molina.

1701
Felipe V of Bourbon enters Madrid; the first ruler of a united Spain, the 17-year-old from France speaks no Spanish.

Court painter Diego de Velázquez was a superstar of Spain's Golden Age, despite his uncompromisingly realistic style

1738
The first stone is laid for the Palacio Real (Royal Palace). It is finished in 1764.

1759
Carlos III ascends the throne. Nicknamed the 'best Lord Mayor of Madrid', he commissions grand buildings that are now home to the Museo del Prado and the Museo Nacional Centro de Arte Reina Sofía.

1793
Diario de Madrid runs the first newspaper report of a bullfight.

1808
Napoleon's forces occupy Madrid. Napoleon's brother, Joseph Bonaparte, is named King José I of Spain. The annual 2 May holiday (*2 de mayo*) commemorates the Madrid uprising against the French, which also inspires two famous paintings by Goya (now in the Prado).

1814
Madrid is restored to Spanish rule under King Fernando VII.

1819
The Museo del Prado opens to the public.

1879
The PSOE (Spanish Socialist Party) is founded at the Casa Labra bar in Madrid.

1900
The city has one million inhabitants.

1919
The Metro is inaugurated by Alfonso XIII.

1931
Republicans sweep the elections and King Alfonso XIII steps down.

1936–9
The Spanish Civil War takes place. Republican Madrid is besieged by Franco's Nationalist army for three years.

1946
United Nations sanctions against the Franco regime begin. Sanctions remain until 1955.

1960
The city has 2.2 million inhabitants.

1975
Franco dies and Juan Carlos I is Spain's first king since 1931. Modernisation of the city begins.

1981
Spain's democracy is threatened by a military coup. Order is restored by Juan Carlos I.

1986
Spain joins the EEC (EU).

1992
Madrid is named as the European Capital of Cultur

1998
Alcalá de Henares is declared a UNESCO Worl Heritage Site.

2002
The Euro replaces the *peseta* as the national currency of Spain.

2004
Madrid mourns after 191 people are killed and man more injured by train bom on March 11.

Romantic view of Franco's capture of Madrid (1939)

Peace & Quiet

Two's company in leafy Retiro Park

Around every corner in Madrid there is a bench or a small square to rest weary feet or eat a sandwich. In addition, the famous Parque del Retiro (➤ 24), is by no means the only green space in which to find peace and quiet.

Casa de Campo

To the west of the city, on the far side of the Río Manzanares, this vast park includes cafeterias, tennis courts, swimming pools, a lake, a zoo and the Parque de Atracciones (amusement park). The former hunting grounds are ideal for a picnic, kicking a ball about, or even tramping through the scrubland. During the Civil War, Franco's troops were based here, and some signs of the trenches are still visible. The most fun way to get there is by the Teleférico (➤ 71), but you can also go by Metro (Batán, Lago,) or drive there. Some parking places have become popular meeting spots for the gay community and prostitution is rife. It is best avoided at night.

A lazy Retiro Park afternoon

Campo del Moro

Just below the Palacio Real, this park is more like a wood, even though the design is formal, with pleasant avenues and two attractive fountains – Las Conchas and Los Tritones. The royal carriage horses trot through for their daily exercise at noon.

Real Jardín Botánico

A step away from the Prado and the *paseos*, this relaxing spot has stunning displays of flowers and shrubs (➤ 70). As this is still a centre for scientific research, don't expect cafeterias or refreshments for sale. The entrance is on the Plaza de Murillo.

Jardines de Sabatini

Just north of the Palacio Real, these formal gardens were only laid out in the 1930s. Few visitors come here, so peace and quiet are guaranteed for most of the day. However, it is popular with mothers and small children after school.

Parque del Oeste

Set into the side of a hill, this rectangular park northwest of the Palacio Real has recently been renovated. The broad and elegant Paseo del Pintor Rosales runs along one side; the Ermita de San Antonio de la Florida (➤ 39) stands at the bottom of the slope. At the southern end is La Rosaleda, a rose garden which is at its best in May, and the Parque de la Montaña. Its temple was a gift from the Egyptian government. This is also the start of the Teleférico (➤ 71). The park is best avoided at night.

Plaza de Vázquez de Mella.

North of the Gran Vía, near the Telefónica (➤ 71), this refurbished square has benches, a fountain and a small playground where youngsters can burn off surplus energy.

Hotel Ritz

For a special treat, there is nothing quite like tea in the sheltered, flower-filled garden of one of the city's great hotels (➤ 102). It is a few steps north of the Prado (➤ 26).

Cooling off: Retiro fountain

There is always somewhere shady to rest your feet

Madrid's Famous

Carlos III

One king can be thanked for the grand buildings, parks and art galleries of Madrid: Carlos III (1716–88). He opened the Parque del Retiro (➤ 24) and its observatory and commissioned the building which now houses the Prado (➤ 26), the Real Jardín Botánico next door (➤ 70), and the elegant fountains along the *paseos* (➤ 59). The ordinary folk of the city also benefitted from a sewage and refuse system, as well as streets that were both paved and lit. No wonder he is remembered as the *Rey-Alcalde* (the King-Mayor) – perhaps the best mayor the city has ever had.

Goya

Every church and museum in Madrid worth its salt has a painting or fresco by Francisco José de Goya y Lucientes (1746–1828). A native of Aragón, his talent was soon recognised in Madrid. In 1792, a serious illness left him deaf and also gave a new, hard edge to his work. By 1799, he was court artist to Carlos IV, but his portraits of the royal family were never flattering. As he grew older, he painted his most haunting works. His record of the French massacres in Madrid on 2 and 3 May in 1808, and the despairing 'Black Pictures' are a highlight of the Prado (➤ 26).

Juan Carlos I, King of Spain since 1975

Juan Carlos I

When Alfonso XIII abdicated in 1931 in favour of the Republic, few believed that Spain would ever have a king again. However, when General Franco died in 1975, Spain reverted to a monarchy. Juan Carlos was born in exile in Rome in 1938. In 1981 his forceful intervention to prevent a military coup endeared him to the Spanish people who celebrated the royal jubilee in 2000 with heartfelt enthusiasm. In May 2004 there were further celebrations when Prince Felipe, eldest son of Juan Carlos and Queen Sofia, married former TV journalist, Letizia Ortiz.

Top Ten

Above: *mirror image –
Museo Nacional Centro
de Arte Reina Sofía*
Right: *Felipe III's statue
in the Plaza Mayor*

15

1

Monasterio de las Descalzas Reales

www.patrimonionacional.es/
descreal/descreal.htm

 40C3

 Plaza de las Descalzas Reales 3

 91 454 8800

Tue–Sat 10:30–12:45, 4–5:45, Sun, public hols 11–1:45. Closed Fri PM, all day Mon

Plenty near by (€)

Callao, Sol, Opera

All routes to Puerta del Sol

Plaza Mayor 3
91 588 16 36

 None

Moderate; free Wed to EU citizens

 Puerta del Sol (➤ 64)

Visit by tour only, tours every 20 min, duration 45 min

Staircase in the Monasterio de las Descalzas Reales

Visit this 16th–century convent, still a closed order, not just to admire the notable art collection, but also to soak up the medieval atmosphere.

Behind the austere brick and stone façade, some 25 brown-robed nuns go about their quiet daily life. Opening hours are limited, so expect to queue. Groups are ushered in 20 at a time for a basic tour of the convent, which was founded in 1559 by Juana de Austria, daughter of Carlos V. The convent houses the Descalzas Reales (Barefoot Royal Sisters), women who initially came from the royal family and nobility (modern nuns are generally of humbler origin). As a dowry, each brought fine religious works of art by European masters such as Titian, Brueghel the Elder, van Eyck and Zurbarán.

The tour begins in the cloisters, then climbs the massive staircase past walls painted by Ximénez Donoso and Claudio Coello. The broad stone balustrade is carved from a single piece of granite. At the top, Felipe IV and the rest of the royal family look down from their painted balcony. All around the upper cloister are 16 elaborate chapels, the most important of which is dedicated to Virgen de Guadelupe. Don't miss the doll's house-like altar in one corner, designed to teach children about the sacred vessels used during Mass. In what was once the nuns' dormitory is the restored Salón de Tapices, hung with sumptuous Flemish tapestries based on Rubens' cartoons. Peek out of the window at the kitchen garden, still tended by the sisters, even though they are overlooked by office blocks.

2
Museo de América

This museum's outstanding collection focuses on the art and culture of the Americas from before the Spanish colonial period to the present day.

If this museum were located on the Paseo del Prado, it would be packed with visitors. Set in the university district northwest of the city centre, it remains a well-kept secret. The spacious building has two floors of permanent exhibits, divided into five sections: Instruments of Knowledge, the American Reality, Society, Religion and Communication. Maps explain the movements of native peoples through the Americas and the routes of the explorers; feathered head-dresses contrast with ceramic vessels shaped like sting rays or parrots.

Since the Spanish melted down much of the gold they found in the Americas, the surviving Quimbayas treasure is particularly important. Dating from 600 BC–AD 600, the 130 gold objects were discovered in two tombs in Colombia. Finely-crafted, they range from statuettes and bowls to necklaces and helmets. There is even a whistle and a trumpet.

Equally important are the codices, or manuscripts, which are keys to understanding pre-Colombian culture. One of only three surviving Mayan manuscripts is the *TroCortesiano Codex*, with symbols depicting the religious rituals of the Mayan calendar. Although the *Tudela Codex* also records religious ceremonies – this time of the late Aztec culture – it is post-conquest and dates from 1553. Written on paper and bound like a book, it is annotated in Spanish.

Paintings from the Spanish colonial period also serve as historical records, ranging from a large work showing the Archbishop and Viceroy Morcillo entering the city of Potosí (modern Bolivia) to a series of portraits of the multi-racial society of Mexico.

66A5

Avenida de los Reyes Católicos 6

91 543 94 37/91 549 26 41

Tue–Sat 9:30–3; Sun, public hols 10–3

Café (€)

Moncloa

1, 12, 16, 44, 61, 82, 83, 132, 133

Plaza Mayor 3
91 588 16 36

Good

Cheap; free under-18, over-65; Sun

Teleférico (► 71)

Lectures Sat at 12 (except Aug)

Above: *aerial view*
Below: *Quimbaya gold statue (AD 200–1000)*

17

3
Museo Lázaro Galdiano

Banker Lázaro Galdiano left his home and collection to the city

www.flg.es

 67E5

Calle de Serrano 122

91 561 60 84

Wed–Mon 10–4:30

Plenty near by (€)

Rubén Darío, Núñez del Balboa Gregorio

12, 16, 51, 61

Calle del Duque de Medinaceli 2
91 429 49 51

 Good

Cheap; free under-18, over-65, Wed

 Museo Sorolla (► 20)

Free guided tour noon daily. Extra opening during *Noches de Museo* (museum nights) Thu 7:30PM–11PM, end Jun to mid-Oct

The former home of publisher and collector José Lázaro Galdiano (1872–1947) contains dazzling paintings and priceless objets d'art.

The neo-Renaissance *palazzo*, the Parque Florido, has re-opened after a comprehensive programme of restoration and refurbishment. The exhibition begins on the ground floor with an assessment of Lázaro's intentions and achievments and offers a taster of what lies in store. Rare books and manuscripts, exquisite caskets of enameled wood, gold and silverware, rock crystal and gemstones, medieval stained glass and Renaissance bronzes all vie for attention. Look out for El Greco's magnificent *Adoration of the Magi* (room 2) and the 15th-century sword presented to Pope Innocent VIII by the Count of Tendilla (room 3).

Spanish paintings and scultpure are on the first floor in the former private apartments. Apart from the triptychs and panel paintings by medieval masters like Bartolome de Castro, there are canvases by El Greco, Murillo, Zurbarán, José de Ribera, Velázquez and Luís Paret. Don't miss Goya's spooky *Witches Sabath* (Cabinete) and in the adjoining room (13) the Godoy table, fashioned from mahogany, marble and gilded bronze in 1800. The second floor is devoted to European Art from the 15th to the 19th centuries. Most of the major schools are represented and there are works by Quentin Metsys, Hieronymous Bosch, Breughel the Younger, Cranach, Dürer, Rembrandt, van Dyck and Tiepolo among the displays of Limoges enamels, Sèvres porcelain, cut glass, ivories, French table clocks and miniatures. Admirers of Constable, Gainsborough, Lawrence and Sir Joshua Reynolds are in for a treat.

4

Museo Nacional Centro de Arte Reina Sofía

One of the largest buildings in Europe houses Spain's national museum of modern art, including the world-famous painting, Guernica *by Picasso.*

Picasso's protest: Guernica was bombed in the Spanish Civil War

The two glass elevators slide up and down the outside of what was an 18th-century hospital. Two floors are devoted to the permanent collection of paintings and sculptures from the late 19th century to the present day; two more have temporary exhibitions along with Jean Nouvel's brand new 27,000sq m annex which opened in 2004..

Start up on the fourth floor. Rooms 34 and 35 are dominated by the gigantic canvases of Robert Motherwell (USA) and Antoni Tàpies (Spain). Pablo Palazuelo's geometric patterns make your eyes ache, while his fellow-*madrileño*, Eduardo Arroyo, prefers a big, bright palette. A star of the contemporary sculpture scene is Eduardo Chillida, whose massive metal works fill Rooms 42 and 43.

The biggest crowds are on the second floor. As you approach Rooms 6 and 7, you can hear the hum of conversation in the rooms dedicated to Picasso. The main focus is *Guernica* (1937), Picasso's powerful work condemning the unjustifiable bombing of the Basque town of Guernica during the Spanish Civil War. Picasso's will stated that the painting could only be brought to Spain when democracy was restored. In 1981, six years after Franco's death, *Guernica* was finally shown in Spain.

It is not the only politically inspired painting on display here. Rooms 10 and 11 are devoted to Dalí, whose *Enigma of Hitler* (1939) also reflects the uncertainty of those times. Nearby rooms feature works by Juan Miró, Juan Gris and the surrealist painters Max Ernst and René Magritte.

www.museoreinasofia.mcu.es

✚ 41E1

✉ Calle Santa Isabel 52

☎ 91 467 50 62

🕐 Mon, Wed–Sat 10–9, Sun 10–2:30

🍴 Restaurant/café (€)

Ⓜ Atocha

🚌 All routes to Atocha

♿ Good

💲 Cheap; free under-18, over-65; Sat 2:30–9, Sun

↔ Museo Nacional de Antropología (➤ 49), Museo Thyssen-Bornemisza (➤ 22), Museo del Prado (➤ 26)

❓ The *Abono Paseo del Arte* ticket is a reduced rate, combined ticket (➤ 22, panel)

5
Museo Sorolla

www.mcu.es/nmuseos/
sorolla

67D5

Paseo del General
Martínez Campos 37

91 310 15 84

Tue–Sat 10–3, Sun,
public hols 10–2

Plenty near by (€)

Iglesia, Rubén Darío

5, 16, 61

Calle del Duque de
Medinaceli 2
902 100 007

None

Cheap; free for under
18s, over 65s and
Sun AM

Museo Lázaro Galdiano
(▶ 18)

*The museum's garden is
decorated with carefully
sited statues*

*A well-furnished mansion, a fine art gallery and a
painter's studio all in one, the home of Joaquín
Sorolla (1863–1923) is a gem.*

With its Moorish gardens and trickling fountains, the
atmosphere at the recently refurbished Museo Sorolla is in
total contrast to the formality and grandeur of Madrid's
major museums. Born in Valencia, Sorolla worked in Paris
and Rome before becoming the darling of European and
American high society. Often labelled 'the Spanish
Impressionist', Sorolla had no connection with that
movement. Passionate about Spain and the Spanish, his
treatment of sharp light and heavy shade was both
individual and highly accomplished. While he lived in
Madrid (1910–23), his large paintings, with their bold and
lively brushwork of people in sun-dappled landscapes,
were in great demand.

In the first room you
see the romantic side of
Sorolla. Don't miss *Madre*
(1895), a simple scene of a
tired mother and her new-
born. Then walk through
the second room with its
jolly beach scenes to
Sorolla's studio. Here the
soaring walls are covered
in canvases, including
several of his wife, Clotilde.

Sorolla's finest work is
upstairs. His studies for a
series for the Hispanic
Society of New York
include rustic types in
colourful regional costume,
a bagpiper and a Don
Quixote lookalike fron La
Mancha, complete with
donkey and windmills and
a large painting of four
women taking a siesta. In
galleries on the ground
floor (enter from the
garden) is Sorolla's fine
collection of antique
Spanish pottery, as well as
some lively sketches of
Central Park, New York.

Sorolla's antique pottery collection

Sorolla recorded Spanish folklore for a New York club

6
Museo Thyssen-Bornemisza

The Thyssen–Bornemisza family built the world's finest art collection. It moved to Madrid in 1992, completing the city's golden triangle of museums.

The Thyssen-Bornemisza collection's elegant 18th-century home

www.museothyssen.org

 41E3

Paseo del Prado 8

91 369 01 51

Tue–Sun 10–7. Closed New Year

Restaurant/café (€)

Banco de España

1, 2, 5, 9, 10, 14, 15, 20, 27, 34, 37, 45, 51, 52, 53, 74, 146, 150

 Calle del Duque de Medinaceli 2
902 100 007

Very good

 Moderate, reduction for children over 12 and over 65s

 Museo Nacional Centro de Arte Reina Sofía (► 19), Museo del Prado (► 26)

 Less crowded Wed–Fri lunchtime. Temporary exhibitions, café open until midnight Jul, Aug. The *Abono Paseo del Arte* ticket is a reduced rate ticket for the Prado, Museo Thyssen-Bornemisza and Museo Nacional Centro de Arte Reina Sofía

Sympathetically remodelled, the spacious 19th-century Palacio de Villahermosa is the perfect setting for an art history lesson spanning seven centuries of European and American art. The lesson begins on the top floor, where the 13th– to 15th-century religious works positively glow, thanks to excellent lighting. Next come a succession of fascinating early Renaissance portraits. In Room 5, near Hans Holbein the Younger's classic portrait of Henry VIII of England, is Francesco Cossa's intriguing 15th-century *Portrait of a Man*. This is an experiment in *trompe l'oeil* and perspective as a hand holds out a ring for you to inspect. Room 20 has two Flemish masterpieces, lit as fiercely as a movie set: *Esau selling his Birthright* (1627) by Hendrik Terbrugghen and *Supper at Emmaus* (1633) by Matthias Stom.

On through the centuries, the tour continues past Titian and Caravaggio, Impressionists and Expressionists. On the ground floor are eight rooms of 20th-century works. In Room 41, works by Picasso and Braque exemplify the technical and aesthetic revolution of Cubism. Room 45 is lined with familiar 20th-century works: Picasso's *Harlequin with a mirror* (1923), Chagall's *Rooster*, a rich blue Miró titled *Catalan peasant with a Guitar*, plus others by Braque, Léger, Kandinsky, Ernst and Madrid's own Juan Gris. Room 47 focuses on star American names such as Edward Hopper, whose *Hotel Room* (1931) has a typically lonely and mysterious atmosphere. The new glass pavilion houses 19th- and 20th-century paintings from the collection of Baroness Carmen Thyssen-Bornemisza.

7
Palacio Real

With a grand parade ground, fabulous views over the city, imposing staircases and ornate rooms, this is everything that a royal palace should be.

The regal façade of the Palacio Real

All that is missing is the royal family, who prefer to live in the Zarzuela Palace on the outskirts of Madrid. Today, the grand 250-year-old Palacio Real is used solely for state occasions. To get the most out of your visit, join a 45-minute tour, then wander round at your leisure. As you climb the main staircase, imagine the red carpet treatment and guard of honour that greets new ambassadors and visiting heads of state. Each room seems more magnificent than the last. With its backdrop of 17th-century Flemish tapestries, the Sala de Columnas is often used for ceremonies, such as Spain's entry to the European Community (1986) and the Middle East peace accord (1992). Curiously, no one sits on the two thrones in the Throne Room because King Juan Carlos and Queen Sofía prefer to stand during audiences. Continue past great paintings by Goya and admire ornate clocks, then prepare yourself for Gasparini's Robing Room. This jewel box of a room, with a marble floor, decorated walls and encrusted ceiling, is now used for taking coffee after state banquets.

The banqueting hall has a grand ceiling fresco of Christopher Columbus offering the world to the *Reyes Católicos*, Fernando and Isabel. Outside the palace, the Real Armería (Royal Armoury) has undergone a facelift, installing the latest museum technology for its world-class collection. Temporary exhibitions are also held; most are free, with direct access from the street. Visitor-friendly improvements such as a cafeteria and toilets have also been installed. The Real Farmacia (Royal Pharmacy), near the Armoury, is also well worth a visit.

www.patrimonionacional.es

🞥 40A3

✉ Calle Bailén s/n

☎ 91 454 88 00

🕐 Summer: Mon–Sat 9–6, Sun, public hols 9–3. Winter: Mon–Sat 9:30–5, Sun, public hols 9–2. Closed on offical occasions

🍴 Cafeteria (€)

Ⓜ Opera

🚌 3, 148

ℹ Plaza Mayor 3
☎ 91 588 16 36

♿ Good

✋ Moderate

↔ Monasterio de la Encarnación (► 48)

❓ Multilingual guided tours. Changing of the Guard at 12, 1st Wed of month Feb–May, Sep–Dec. Telephone to confirm.

8
Parque del Retiro

The Palacio de Cristal (Crystal Palace) in Retiro Park

The 130ha park, with its mixture of formal gardens, tree-studded lawns and a large lake, acts as a set of lungs to refresh the city centre.

 41F2

 Calle de Alfonso XII

Jun–Sep 6:30AM–midnight; Oct–May 6AM–10PM

 Plenty (€)

Atocha, Ibiza, Retiro

All routes to Retiro

 Calle del Duque de Medinaceli 2
☎ 902 100 007

Good

 Free

Casón del Buen Retiro (➤ 36), Museo Nacional de Artes Decorativas (➤ 50)

Felipe IV created this Buen Retiro (a pleasant place to retire or retreat) in the 17th century. This is where the court came to have fun, staying in the Buen Retiro Palace and watching bullfights, plays and fireworks in the gardens. A century later, Carlos III opened the royal park to the public – as long as they were dressed properly. By the mid-19th century, anyone could enjoy the park, whatever their garb.

Nowadays, a Sunday stroll is a must. *Madrileños* promenade along the Paseo del Estanque, while children play and watch noisy puppet shows. Take in a free concert of *zarzuela* music at the Templete de la Musica, have your portrait sketched or try your luck at the roulette wheels of the *chulapos*, colourful locals in waistcoats and caps. There are pathways for cyclists and rollerbladers, shady spots for picnicking and formal parterres with botanical name-plates to identify the species.

Important landmarks include the elaborate 1922 memorial and statue of Alfonso XII, *El Pacificador* (the Peacemaker), which overlooks the *estanque* (lake). Check whether there are any exhibitions in the two glass halls, the Palacio de Cristal and Palacio de Velázquez, both built in the 1880s, or the restored Casa de Vacas (House of Cows), which is on the site of an old dairy. La Rosaleda (Rose Garden) is at its best in May. Avoid the park after dark.

9
Plaza Mayor

Traffic-free and large enough to swallow a crowd of 50,000, one of the most handsome squares in Europe is dominated by a royal statue.

Felipe III's statue is a handy rendezvous spot on the Plaza Mayor

The bronze equestrian statue of Felipe III makes a popular meeting point. The reliefs around the four giant lampposts spell out the history of the plaza. In 1617, under Felipe III, the old square was replaced by this new arena, created to hold everything from bullfights to theatre, festivals to inquisitions. Its inauguration coincided with the beatification of San Isidro, Madrid's patron saint, in 1620, and the spacious balconies have been hired out to spectators ever since.

Throughout the year, tourists and locals alike watch the world go by from café tables that spill across the paving stones. During the annual San Isidro festivities in May, giant *cocidos* (stews) and *paellas* are served up, and in summer there are concerts and plays. The annual Christmas market, with its traditional sweets, cakes and toys, has been a feature since 1837. The Casa de la Panadería, the dominant building on the north side, dates from 1590, but the jolly murals were only added in 1992. The oldest shop on the square is Bustillo (No 4), where they have been selling cloth since 1790.

Sunday mornings are special. Since 1927, the arcades have been filled with dozens of tables for the popular stamp and coin collectors' market. In fact, anything that can be collected is displayed and offered for sale: postcards, cheese labels, pins and lottery tickets.

✚ 40C3

✉ Plaza Mayor

🍴 Botín (€), cafés near by (€)

Ⓜ Sol, La Latina

🚌 All routes to Sol

ℹ Plaza Mayor 3
☎ 91 588 16 36

♿ Very good

✋ Free

↔ Casa de la Villa (➤ 36), Basílica de San Miguel (➤ 32), Botín (➤ 33)

10
Museo del Prado

A Prado highlight: Las Hilanderas *(The Spinners) by Velázquez (c1657)*

www.museoprado.mcu.es

 41E2

 Paseo del Prado s/n

 91 330 28 00, 24hr phone; 906 322 222

Tue–Sun 9–7, public hols 9–2. Closed Mon, 1 Jan, Good Friday, 1 May, 25 Dec

 Restaurant/café (€)

Atocha, Banco de España

 9, 10, 14, 19, 27, 34, 37, 45

Calle del Duque de Medinaceli 2
902 100 007

Good

Cheap; free under-18s, over-65s; Sun 9–7

 Museo Nacional Centro de Arte Reina Sofía (► 19), Museo Thyssen-Bornemisza (► 22)

Abono Paseo del Arte ticket: reduced rate for Prado, Museo Thyssen-Bornemisza and Museo Nacional Centro de Arte Reina Sofía. For the latest changes at the Prado, check their website above

> *One of the world's great museums, Museo del Prado is reorganizing its vast collection by expanding into three nearby buildings.*

The Edificio Villanueva on the Paseo del Prado will continue to house masterpieces by Bosch, Goya, El Greco, Murillo, Rubens, Titian, Velázquez and Zurbarán. Near by, the Antiguo Salón de Reinos will have 18th-century art and the Casón del Buen Retiro, modern masters. This and Rafael Moneo's new building, incorporating the cloisters of the Jerónimos Monastery, opened in 2004. To get the best out of a visit, focus on a favourite artist or era.

Not surprisingly, the range of Spanish art from the 11th to the 19th century is unparalleled, especially from the *Siglo de Oro*, the golden 17th century. Foremost was Velázquez (1599–1660), court painter to Felipe IV. His works, such as *Las Meninas* (The Maids of Honour) and *Las Hilanderas* (The Spinners) are turning points in the art of composition. A century later, Goya (1746–1828) was, arguably, even more influential. His range was extraordinary, from his naked *Maja* (Courtesan) to the *Fusilamientos del 3 de mayo*. This patriotic, passionate painting commemorates the heroism of the *madrileño* revolt against the French invaders in May 1808. Most disturbing of all are his 14 *Pinturas Negras* (Black Paintings) from the end of his life. *Saturn devouring one of his sons* and *Witches' Sabbath* make anything but comfortable viewing.

Don't miss *The Garden of Delights* by the Flemish master Hieronymus Bosch (1450–1516). Despite years of academic study, this allegorical triptych portraying human frailties has yet to be fully deciphered.

What to See

Above: hand-painted tiles still mark ancient streets
Right: the bull is a popular symbol all over Spain

CALLE
MAYOR

*Hand-painted tiles at the
Fontanilla restaurant*

MADRID ENVIRONS

Loma del Corcho   M60

El Pardo

Río Manzanares

FUE

3
Segovia

A6

TETUÁN
Estadio
Santiago
Bernabéu

Aravaca

M613

M500

MONCLOA

Pozuelo
de Alarcón

M40

M30

M503

CHAMBERÍ
Palacio
de Liria

Humera   Casa
de Campo

2 • La Cabana   Somosaguas   **Parque de
Atracciones**

Palacio
Real
CENTRO

Monte   Prado de   M602   Parque   Museo
Príncipe   Somosaguas   Zoológico   del Prado

ARGANZUELA

Los
Retamares   LATINA

NV E90

CARABANCHEL   M401

1   NV
Badajoz   M40   VILLAVERDE

N401

NV

E905

Alcorcón

Leganés

A   B

Fresh fruit and vegetables for sale in Calle de Serrano

View over the Campo del Moro from the Palacio Real

Madrid

Back in the 1990s Madrid seemed forever destined to play second fiddle to its perennial rival, Barcelona. Even while the capital was enjoying its role as European City of Culture in 1992, most eyes were focused on Barcelona, then hosting the Olympic Games. Since the dawning of the new millennium, however, Madrid has discovered a dynamism previously lacking with the launch of its own ambitious bid to stage the 2012 Games. Meanwhile all three major art galleries are expanding, there are radical plans to remodel the Paseo del Prado, the metro is growing at a phenomenal rate and Barajas airport will double its operational capacity by 2005. Yet despite Madrid's increasingly forward-looking image Archibald Lyall's observation from the 1960s, that Madrid was both the most Spanish and the least Spanish city on the peninsula, still rings true.

> *' … the least Spanish because it is the most modernised and international, and the most Spanish because …of the mixed population which has flowed into it from various regions of Spain, it is a synthesis of them all. '*

ARCHIBALD LYALL
Well Met in Madrid (1960)

Madrid

Like Piccadilly Circus in London or Times Square in New York, Madrid has its own heartbeat: the Puerta del Sol. This is the focus of the old city, which is bordered by the Palacio Real to the west and the Paseo del Prado to the east. On or near this leafy boulevard are the city's three world-famous museums of art.

The northern boundary of the old quarter is the 100-year-old Gran Vía, while around the southern perimeter a loop of broad roads joins the Puerta de Toledo and the Glorieta de los Embajadores. Within this relatively small area are narrow, medieval streets and alleyways, massive churches and a host of bars and restaurants.

Madrid's lungs are to the east and west. Beyond the Prado (► 26) is the Parque del Retiro (► 24) with its formal paths and gardens; beyond the Palacio Real is the Casa de Campo, a vast park with a lake and recreation area. North of the Gran Vía is another network of old streets, including the Chueca district. Usually labelled as Madrid's gay area, this is open to all and has many trendy restaurants. To the northeast, the Salamanca district is Madrid at its most affluent, with expensive apartments and elegant shops overlooking tree-lined streets.

With few skyscrapers, Madrid does not overwhelm the visitor, and as the renovation of old buildings continues, the capital is looking better than ever. It is a compact city, so whether you walk or take the Metro, you can see and do a lot in a relatively short time.

The Casa de la Panadería on the Plaza Mayor

Cool cloisters line the Plaza Mayor

31

CALLE MAYOR

The ornate Basilica de San Miguel

What to See in Madrid

BASILICA DE SAN FRANCISCO EL GRANDE ✪

A long-term restoration programme inside this vast 18th-century church, which stands on the site of a hermitage built by San Francisco (St Francis of Assisi) in 1217, is now complete. Guides show you the highlights of a building that has served as a church, national pantheon and even an army barracks. Joseph Bonaparte, the upstart king of Spain, wanted to use it as the parliament building. The enormous dome measuring 33m across is covered with 19th-century frescos. In the very first chapel to the left of the main entrance is *The Sermon of San Bernardino of Siena* (1781) by Goya. He produced this unremarkable work at the age of 35, long before the dramatic canvases that are a highlight of the Prado (➤ 26). Even in his early career, Goya put himself into his paintings; here he is the one in yellow, on the right-hand side. Behind the altar is the Sala Capitular, with its carved wooden seats and paintings by 17th-century Spanish masters such as Francisco Zurbarán and Alonso Cano.

BASILICA DE SAN MIGUEL ✪

One of Madrid's true baroque churches (1739–49), San Miguel was squeezed on to the small plot of ground that once held the church of San Justo. Architect Santiago Bonavía used several design tricks to give the interior the appearance of more space. In the narrow street, the exterior, with its elegant curved façade, statues and bells, also looks bigger. The consistency of the baroque design reflects Bonavía's Italian roots.

✚ 40A1
⊠ Calle de San Buenaventura 1
☎ 91 365 38 00
⏰ Tue–Sat 11–1, 5–7. Closed public hols
🍴 Plenty near by (€)
Ⓜ Puerta de Toledo, La Latina
♿ Ramp
💰 Cheap
↔ Iglesia de San Andrés (➤ 45)
❓ Guided tour only

✚ 40B2
⊠ Calle de San Justo 4
☎ 91 548 40 11
⏰ Open Mon–Sat 11–12:15, 5:30–7 and for Mass
🍴 Botín (➤ 33)
Ⓜ Sol, Opera, Tirso de Molina
♿ None 💰 Free

BOTÍN ✪

Peer down the steps leading out of the southwest corner of the Plaza Mayor and you see what is, according to the *Guinness Book of Records*, the oldest restaurant business in the world. The descendants of Jean Botín, a French cook, ran a restaurant near by on the Plaza de Herradores until fire destroyed the premises in the 1940s. The *sobrinos* (cousins) took over the present establishment, which dates back to 1725. Each dining-room reeks with atmosphere. One was the 16th-century *bodega* (wine cellar) and has arched brick walls; the others have dark beams and wall tiles. The focal point is the original *horno de asar* (wood-fired oven), hidden behind well-worn antique ceramic tiles. Although the inn has seen a few changes over the centuries, the oven has always been used to roast or bake meat, such as *cochinillo* (roast suckling pig) and *cordero* (milk-fed lamb). After three hours of slow cooking, the meat is so tender you can cut it with a fork. Legend has it that in 1765, the 19-year-old Goya worked at the original Botín, washing dishes. Almost two centuries later, when Ernest Hemingway dined here, the typically *madrileño* dishes were much the same: stuffed pig's trotters, grilled fish, and *cuajada* (curds). Not much has changed today. This remains as much a place for locals as a shrine for foreign visitors.

www.restaurantebotin.com
- 40B3
- ✉ Calle de Cuchilleros 17
- ☎ 91 366 42 17
- ⏰ Daily 1–4, 8–12
- Ⓜ Sol, Tirso de Molina
- ♿ None
- ↔ Plaza Mayor (► 25), Basilica de San Miguel (► 32)
- ❓ Reservation recommended

Botín is the world's oldest restaurant

CALLE MAYOR

🔲 67E4
🍴 Plenty (€–€€)
Ⓜ Serrano, Núñez de Balboa

Below: *you have to be smart even to go window-shopping on chic Calle de Serrano*

www.casamerica.es
🔲 41E4
✉ Paseo de Recoletos 2
☎ 91 595 48 00
Ⓜ Exhibitions: Tue–Sat 11–2, 5–8; Sun and public hols 11–2
🍴 Snack bar, restaurant in Palacio (€–€€)
Ⓜ Banco de España
♿ Good
✋ Free/cheap (exhibitions)
↔ Palacio de Comunicaciones (➤ 57), Plaza de la Cibeles (➤ 62)
❓ Shop sells Latin-American handicrafts

CALLE DE SERRANO ✪

Calle de Serrano is synonymous with 'expensive'. Like Fifth Avenue in New York or Bond Street in London, it is *the* place to go shopping for anything beautiful and costly. A broad thoroughfare, Calle de Serrano runs north–south through the elegant Salamanca district, which was laid out in a grid pattern in the late 19th century. Over the years, nearby streets have also sprouted fine shops. Stroll down Calle de Claudio Coello, parallel to Serrano, and explore cross streets such as Calle de Jorge Juan, Calle de Goya and Calle de José Ortega y Gasset, where limousines, their engines ticking over, wait outside designer boutiques.

CASA DE AMÉRICA ✪

In Spanish, the word 'América' tends to refer to Latin America rather than to the USA. Ties between Spain and her former colonies remain strong, and this lively cultural centre celebrates that connection. Since opening in 1992, it has hosted a wide range of exhibitions, concerts, films and events reflecting Latin-American culture.

Next door is the elaborately decorated 19th-century Palacio de Linares. Supposedly haunted, it was the home of a wealthy financier whose son fell in love with a shop girl. Sent away to England, he returned to Madrid on his father's death. The couple married, but later discovered a letter explaining that the girl was the financier's illegitimate daughter. Pope León XIII told them that they could remain together but must be chaste. Their unhappy ghosts are said to inhabit the mansion.

CASA MUSEO DE LOPE DE VEGA ✪✪

Author of some 2,000 plays, Lope de Vega (1562–1635) was Spain's greatest playwright, penning an estimated 21 million lines. Capable of reading Latin at five, he wrote his first four-act play at the age of 12. This indefatigable genius also enlisted in the Spanish Navy (the Armada), was personal secretary to four aristocrats and had several wives and many children. Although he decided to become a priest in 1614, this had little effect on his love life. Lope lived in this house for the last 25 years of his life, and although only a few items are believed to be his, the author's detailed will enabled experts to refurnish the house much as he knew it.

The garden and vegetable patch of this two-storey, half-timbered shrine have been restored to fit a description in one of his poems: two trees, 10 flowers, two vines, an orange tree and a musk rose. Over the front door is the lintel found when cleaning out the well. The inscription reads *Parva propria magna, magna aliena parva* (To me, my small home is big; to me, other people's large homes are small). The guided tours are led by enthusiastic students. As well as finding out about one of Spain's most renowned authors, you also get some idea of everyday life in a well-off family home in the early 17th century. Note the women's sitting-room where cushions are spread on the *estrado*, a small, Moorish-style dais.

🔢 41D2
✉ Calle Cervantes 11
☎ 91 429 92 16
🕐 Tue–Fri 9:30–2, Sat 10–2. Closed public hols, Aug
🍴 Plenty near by (€)
Ⓜ Antón Martín
♿ None
💶 Cheap, reductions for children under 10s and over 65s
↔ Iglesia y Convento de las Trinitarias (➤ 46)
❓ Guided tour only

Above: *Lope de Vega still haunts his study*

35

Right: *the Casa de Cisneros on the Plaza de la Villa*
Below: *door to the Torre de los Lujanes, Plaza de la Villa*

www.munimadrid.es
+ 40B3
⊠ Plaza de la Villa 5
☎ 91 588 10 0
🕐 Guided tour Mon 5PM
🍴 Plenty near by (€)
Ⓜ Opera, La Latina
♿ Few
💲 Free
↔ Plaza Mayor (➤ 25)

CASA DE LA VILLA ✪✪

Madrid's town hall sits on the Plaza de la Villa, which was a Moorish market place in the 10th and 11th centuries. In this cramped square it is difficult to appreciate the spiked towers and handsome façade that are so typical of 17th-century baroque-Castilian style. The balcony overlooking the Calle Mayor was added in 1789 so that Queen María of Parma could have a better view of the Corpus Christi procession. Opposite the town hall is the oldest surviving private house in Madrid, the 15th-century Casa y Torre de Lujanes. Part Gothic and part Moorish in style, this building is now used by academics. Legend has it that François I of France was imprisoned in the tower after his capture at the Battle of Pavia (1525).

On the south side of the sloping square is the Casa de Cisneros, built by a relative of the powerful Cardinal Cisneros in 1537. Note the façade, which is decorated in the plateresque style, so-called because the intricate carving looks like the work of a *platero* (silversmith). Remodelled in the early 1900s, today it makes an elegant office building for city employees. In the centre of the plaza stands a statue of the great Spanish admiral, the Marqués de Santa Cruz, victor over the Turks at the Battle of Lepanto (1571). The Casa de la Villa is only open to visitors once a week for a guided tour, which is strictly for enthusiasts.

CASÓN DEL BUEN RETIRO ✪✪✪

Closed since 1997, this building is part of the grand plan for the massive reorganisation of the Prado (➤ 26). Along with the nearby Museo del Ejército (Army Museum), it is the only reminder of the grandeur that was once the Buen Retiro Palace, built for Philip IV in the 17th century. *Casón*

www.museoprado.mcu.es
+ 41F3
⊠ Calle Alfonso XII 28, Calle Felipe IV 13
☎ 91 330 28 00

usually means 'big house', but a century ago it was used as a pejorative term to describe the dilapidated structure. When this part of the Prado art complex reopens, it will house 19th-century art.

CATEDRAL DE LA ALMUNDENA ✪

Dedicated to the Virgin of Almundena, Madrid's most important church occupies the same hilltop site as the Palacio Real. The Cathedral de la Almundena was designed by the Marques de Cubas in 1879, but work did not start until 1882 after the plans were changed to resemble a 13th-century cathedral similar to the one at Rheims. The building was eventually completed in the 1980s by architects Fernando Chueca Goitia and Carlos Sidro, who bought a neoclassical influence to the design. The cathedral was finally consecrated by Pope John Paul II in 1993.

In May 2004 the lofty Gothic nave provided a splendid setting for the wedding of the heir to the Spanish throne, Prince Felipe and Doña Letitia Ortiz Rocasolano, a former TV news presenter.

🍴 Plenty near by (€)
🚇 Banco de España, Retiro Atocha
♿ Good
↔ Museo del Prado (➤ 26), Parque del Retiro (➤ 24), Museo Nacional de Artes Decorativas (➤ 50)
❓ Check the building progress on the website on facing page

Above and left: *Casón del Buen Retiro*

✚ 40A3
✉ Calle de Bailén
☎ 91 548 0930
🕐 Daily 10–2, 6–8
🍴 Near by (€)
🚇 Opera
♿ Good
🎫 Free
↔ Palacio Real (➤ 23)

37

40C2
Calle de Toledo 37
91 369 20 37
Daily 8–12, 6:30–8:30.
Closed during services
Plenty near by (€)
La Latina, Tirso de Molina
None
Free
Plaza Mayor (➤ 25),
Botín (➤ 33)

40B5
Calle de Conde Duque 11
91 588 58 34
Exhibitions: Thu–Sat
10–2, 5:30–9, Sun
10:30–2:30
Noviciado, San Bernardo
Varies according to event

40B3
Plaza Conde de Miranda
3
91 548 3901
Mon–Fri 9:30–1, 4–6:30
Plenty near by
Sol
None
Casa de la Villa (➤ 36)

CATEDRAL DE SAN ISIDRO ★

The bulky twin towers of this cathedral were designed to emphasise the importance of the church that is dedicated to Madrid's patron saint. Built between 1622 and 1633, the interior is in the shape of a cross, with the dome above the transept. After Carlos III expelled the Jesuits in 1767, he commissioned the noted architect Ventura Rodríguez to remodel the gloomy interior. For over 200 years, the remains of San Isidro and Santa María de la Cabeza, his equally holy wife, have been venerated here.

CENTRO CULTURAL CONDE DUQUE ★

It is worth checking the entertainment listings to see what is on at this handsome cultural centre. It was once the barracks for the royal bodyguard, and reflected the grandeur of Felipe V's Palacio Real to the south. Begun in 1720, it housed soldiers for 150 years.

Today, it is an important part of Madrid's cultural scene, holding special events and exhibitions throughout the year.

CONVENTO DE LAS CARBONERAS ★★

It is difficult to find this convent. From Plaza de la Villa, step into Calle del Codo and the door is on the right. The nuns belong to a closed order known as the Carboneras (coal cellars), because their painting of the Virgin Mary was found in a coal cellar. The convent is better known in Madrid for selling home-made *dulces* (biscuits) and sweetmeats. This tradition dates back to the 16th century when Santa Teresa of Avila distributed treats made from sugar and egg yolk to the poor. Ring a bell for service; an elaborate serving hatch ensures that the privacy of the nuns is not disturbed.

DID YOU KNOW?

A 200-year-old custom centres on St Anthony, 'the matchmaker'. His feast day on 13 June draws unmarried women to the Ermita. Standing before the baptismal font, each drops 13 pins into the water, presses her palm down and then lifts it out. Each pin sticking to the skin represents a suitor.

ERMITA DE SAN ANTONIO DE LA FLORIDA   ✪✪✪

There are two small churches here: the one on the left is a replica, built to hold services. On the right is the original *ermita*, now a museum dedicated to Goya, one of Spain's greatest artists. The ceiling he painted, revolutionary in technique and subject matter, was a turning point in the history of art and has recently been restored.

Goya was 52 when he began this project in 1798. He had just recovered from a severe illness that left him deaf, but worked from August to mid-December, using brushes, sponges and even his thumbs to portray St Anthony raising a murdered man from the dead. Use the handy mirrors to study the characters: St Anthony, the victim and the man falsely accused of the crime – the saint's own father. This is not an idealised scene with important nobles and ecclesiastics; these are real people showing real emotions, wearing ordinary clothes. It's easy to imagine how this painting shocked the establishment at the time.

www.munimadrid.es/ermita

➕ 66A3

✉ Glorieta de San Antonio de la Florida 5

☎ 91 542 07 22

🕐 Tue–Fri 10–2, 4–8, Sat, Sun 10–2. Closed public hols

🍴 Casa Mingo (next door) (€)

🚇 Príncipe Pío

♿ None

💷 Cheap (free Wed and Sun)

🚡 Teleférico (➤ 71)

❓ Free guided tours (Spanish, English) Sat 11, 12

Opposite page: *Centro Cultural Conde Duque*

Goya's remains are buried in front of the altar in the Ermita de San Antonio de la Florida

CALLE
MAYOR

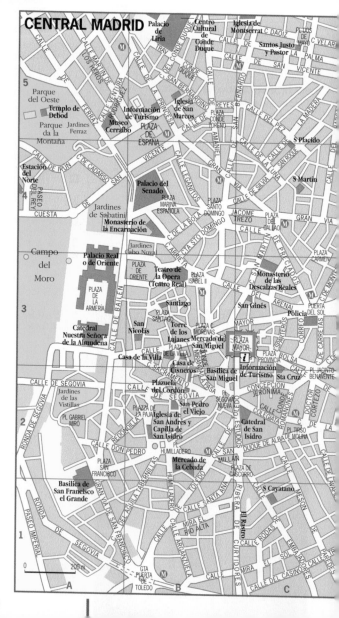

CENTRAL MADRID

Palacio de Liria
Centro Cultural de Conde Duque
Iglesia de Montserrat
Santos Justo y Pastor

Parque del Oeste
Templo de Debod
Información de Turismo
Museo Cerralbo
Iglesia de San Marcos
S Plácido

Parque da la Montaña
Jardines Ferraz
PLAZA DE ESPAÑA

Estación del Norte
Palacio del Senado
S Martín

Jardines de Sabatini
PLAZA MARINA ESPAÑOLA
PLAZA SANTO DOMINGO

Monasterio de la Encarnación

Campo del Moro
Jardines Cabo Noval
Palacio Real o de Oriente
PLAZA DE ORIENTE
Teatro de la Ópera (Teatro Real)
PLAZA ISABEL II
Monasterio de las Descalzas Reales

PLAZA DE LA ARMERÍA
Santiago
PLAZA SANTIAGO
San Ginés
PUERTA DEL SOL
Policía

Catedral Nuestra Señora de la Almudena
San Nicolás
Torre de los Lujanes
Mercado de San Miguel
PLAZA MAYOR

Casa de la Villa
Casa de Cisneros
Basílica de San Miguel
Información de Turismo
Sta Cruz

Jardines de las Vistillas
Plazuela del Cordón
San Pedro el Viejo
Iglesia de San Andrés y Capilla de San Isidro
Catedral de San Isidro

PL GABRIEL MIRÓ
PLAZA SAN FRANCISCO
Mercado de la Cebada

Basílica de San Francisco el Grande
S Cayetano

0   200 m

A   B   C

40

CALLE
MAYOR

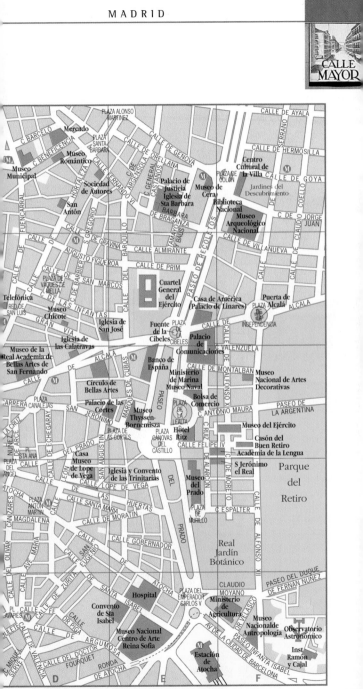

Medieval Madrid

Start at the Plaza Mayor (➤ 25). The steps at the southwest corner lead to the Calle de los Cuchilleros, with its centuries-old mesones (taverns). Cross Plaza de la Puerta Cerrada to Calle de la Cava Baja.

At No 9, La Posada de la Villa dates back to 1642. This quarter retains its historic atmosphere, with tiny shops that still sell basketware and *alpargatas* (rope-soled sandals). At the end, across the Plaza del Humilladero, on the right, is the huge dome of Iglesia de San Andrés (➤ 45).

Walk round the south side and into the Plaza de la Paja.

Once the main square of the medieval city, this was overlooked by a royal palace. Today, a lone statue sits on a bench reading the paper.

Basketware shop on the Calle de la Cava

At the bottom of the square turn right along Calle del Príncipe de Anglona to the 15th-century Iglesia de San Pedro el Viejo, marked by a 14th-century mudéjar (Moorish) tower. Turn left on Travesía del Nuncio and right onto Calle de Segovia.

A plaque at No 1 records the birthplace of San Isidro, Madrid's patron saint. Turn immediately left on Calle del Doctor Letamendi, past the Basilica de San Miguel (➤ 32), along Calle de Puñonrostro and Calle del Codo. Pass the Convento de las Carboneras on the left (➤ 38). Continue to the town hall, the Casa de la Villa (➤ 36).

Turn right, walk back along the Calle Mayor to the Plaza Mayor.

Distance
2km

Time
Half a day with stops

Start/end point
Plaza Mayor
✚ 40C3
Ⓜ Sol

Lunch
Posada de la Villa (€–€€)
✉ Calle de la Cava Baja 9
☎ 91 366 18 60/91
366 18 80

Opposite: *the 17th-century Casa de la Villa (town hall) was designed by Gomez de Mora*

ESTADIO SANTIAGO BERNABÉU (BERNABÉU STADIUM) ⊙⊙

www.realmadrid.com

🔲 28B3

✉ Calle Concha Espina

☎ 91 398 43 00 (stadium),
91 457 06 79 (museum),
902 324 324 (tickets)

🕐 Regular matches during football season. Guided tours in English daily 10:30–6:30 except match days and the following day

🍴 Near by (€)

🚇 Santiago Bernabéu

🚌 14, 27, 40, 43, 120, 147, 150

♿ Good

💲 Expensive (museum)

🛈 Museum (gate 5) open Tue–Sun 10–7:30

Madrid may be crowded with churches, but the most popular modern shrine is this football stadium – the home of Real Madrid. Set on a broad boulevard, with its own Metro station, the 80,000-seat stadium hosted the 1982 World Cup Final. Founded in 1902, 'Real' became one of the most famous football clubs in the world. The name means Royal, and the club has proved to be a dynastic force in football, so much so that in 1998, FIFA, the world governing body, awarded them the accolade, 'the best club in the history of football'.

Even if you can't get to a game, you can experience the atmosphere by visiting the trophy room, right across from the Metro exit or, even better, by joining a guided tour. Visitors are shown a panoramic view of the inside of the stadium, the pitch and players' tunnel, the away dressing room and the trophy room. Crammed with dazzling silver trophies and resonating with screams of *'Gol!, Gol!, Gol!'* this is a football fan's paradise. Numerous video screens show clips from great matches of the past, including their nine European Cup triumphs between 1956 and 2002, as well as 17 Spanish Cups and 29 Spanish league championships. Success is not limited to football: Real participates in many sports. Their basketball team, for example, has an equally glowing history, having won eight European Cups plus the 1981 world club title.

DID YOU KNOW?

Real Madrid are known as the *merengues* (meringues) because of their all-white strip. Rivals Atlético Madrid are the *colchoneros* (mattress makers) because of their red and white striped shirts.

The Bernabeu Stadium

IGLESIA DE LAS CALATRAVAS ✪

In the 17th and 18th centuries the most important street in Madrid was the Calle de Alcalá, which led to the university town of Alcalá de Henares. Facing today's traffic and hemmed in by office blocks, this church is all that is left of the original 17th-century convent of the military order of the Comendadoras of Calatrava, founded by the wives of knights who joined the Crusades. Topped by a fine dome, the massive pink-brick exterior is covered in ornate sculpture. The interior is even more opulent. Here, the focal point in the gloomy light is the massive altarpiece of José Churriguera, the sculptor who lent his name to an exuberant baroque decorative style – Churrigueresque.

IGLESIA DE LAS SALESAS ✪

On the fringes of the atmospheric Chueca district, this massive Baroque church is one of the most impressive in the city. The monastery of the Royal Salesian Order was founded by Barbara of Braganza, the Portuguese wife of Fernando VI, as a spiritual refuge from her domineering mother-in-law, were the king to die before her (as it turned out he outlived her). The church of Santa Bárbara was designed by the French architect, Françoise Carlier, in 1749 and completed nine years later. Pause to admire the elaborately sculpted façade before going inside. Here the highlights are Francesco de Mura's *Visitation* over the high altar, paintings by Corrado Giaquinto, responsible for the frescos in the Palacio Real, and the tombs of Fernando and his wife by Francisco Gutiérrez.

✚ 41D3
✉ Calle de Alcalá 25
☎ 91 521 80 35
🕐 Half hour before Mass (8, 12, 1; Sun 11, 12, 1 & 7)
🍴 Círculo de Bellas Artes (opposite) (€)
🚇 Sevilla
♿ None 👋 Free
↔ Museo de la Real Academia de Bellas Artes de San Fernando (➤ 51)

Above: *Iglesia de las Calatrav*

✚ 41E5
✉ Calle de Bárbara de Braganza 3–5
☎ 91 742 1921
🕐 5–7 and during Mass
🍴 Plenty near by (€)
🚇 Colón
♿ None
👋 Free
↔ Museo Romántico (➤ 56), Museo Arqueológico Nacional (➤ 49)

45

40B2
Plaza de San Andrés 1
91 365 48 71
Mon–Sat 8–12:30, 6–8,
Sun 9–2
Plenty near by (€)
La Latina
None
Free
Catedral de San Isidro
(▶ 37), Basílica de San
Francisco el Grande
(▶ 32)

41D2
Calle de Lope de Vega 18
91 429 56 71
Mon–Fri 8:30AM, Sat 7PM,
Sun 9:30AM, 11:30AM
Plenty near by (€)
Antón Martín
None
Free
Casa Museo Lope de
Vega (▶ 35)

40B3
Plaza de San Miguel
91 541 0792
Mon–Sat 9–2, 5–8
Café del Mercado (€)
Sol
None
Free
Plaza Mayor (▶ 25),
Casa de la Villa (▶ 36)

IGLESIA DE SAN ANDRÉS APÓSTOL

San Andrés is a church with two significant chapels. San Andrés itself, occupying the domed end of the building, reopened in 1998 after years of renovation. Compared with the poorly-lit interiors of most churches, this one is a surprise: bright pink and grey, highlighted with fruit, flowers and angels, like the marzipan on an expensive cake. At the back of San Andrés is the Capilla de San Isidro, which once held the bones of San Isidro, Madrid's patron saint. Beneath the church, renovation continues in the 16th-century Capilla del Obispo (Bishop's Chapel). Closed to the public for restoration, it contains one of the most magnificent Gothic altarpieces in Madrid, a towering, gilded masterpiece attributed to Francisco Giralte.

IGLESIA Y CONVENTO DE LAS TRINITARIAS

The Trinitarias, who wear white cassocks marked with a bold red and blue cross, are a closed order of nuns. In their 17th-century church a plaque commemorates the burial place of Cervantes, author of *Don Quixote*. Each year on 23 April, a memorial service for Spain's most famous writer is held by Spain's Academy of Language. Authors Lope de Vega, Luis de Góngora and Francisco de Quevedo also lived near by and worshipped here. Although the church has fine paintings and a grand altarpiece, the appeal here is to follow in the footsteps of these literary giants. Visiting hours are limited to half an hour before mass, but you are not required to stay for the service itself.

MERCADO DE SAN MIGUEL

This is the only traditional food market of its kind left in the heart of Madrid. Built in 1915 but recently renovated, the hall is a graceful combination of green-painted iron and glass. Even if you are not buying, a stroll past the stalls shows why Madrid is called Spain's biggest port: all the best freshly caught fish is transported straight to the capital. Fishmongers might be working on a

CALLE
MAYOR

whole *mero* (halibut) weighing 40kg; *charcuterías* (delicatessens) are piled with dozens of types of sausage and cheese; *carnicerías* (butchers) offer tender pork; and the range of colourful fresh fruit and vegetables is astonishing. Stop for a snack at the small café-bar in the middle and eavesdrop on vendors discussing deals.

In Madrid terms, this marketplace is relatively new. It dates back to the early 19th century, when José I demolished narrow streets, old houses and ancient churches to create new squares and open spaces in the capital. His enthusiasm earned him the nickname, *El Rey Plazuelas* (King of the Little Squares). The San Miguel market replaced a church of the same name.

Left: *Madrid is jokingly known as Spain's main fishing port*

Food, glorious food, at the Mercado de San Miguel

CALLE MAYOR

The Monasterio de la Encarnación is crammed with treasures

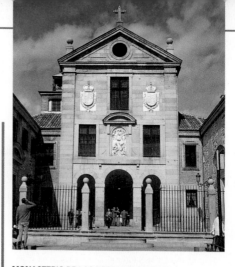

MONASTERIO DE LAS DESCALZAS REALES
(▶ 16, TOP TEN)

MONASTERIO DE LA ENCARNACIÓN ⭐⭐

Another of Madrid's closed orders dedicated to the royal family, this convent is famous on two counts: its collection of some 4,000 *relicarios* (reliquaries) and an annual miracle. Whether you believe that the reliquaries contain the authentic bones of saints or a fragment of the true cross depends on your religious persuasion. However, according to the curator, visitors should appreciate the reliquaries as works of art, created as expressions of religious belief during the 17th century – Spain's Golden Age.

The reliquaries are preserved in glass cases, which line the walls of what looks like a heavily decorated library with an impressive, gilded altar. They come in all shapes and sizes in precious materials of the period, such as coral, marble and crystal, as well as gold and silver. The designs reflect the talents of artists, not just from Spain but also from Germany, the Netherlands, Italy and even the Orient. One of the most venerated reliquaries is a small vial containing a droplet of blood, which is reputedly from the 4th-century physician and martyr, San Pantaleón. On 26 July, the eve of the saint's feast day, the vial is placed on the altar of the church in the convent. There, according to the faithful, *la sangre* (the blood) rematerialises. The convent, still home to a small community of nuns, was founded in 1611 by Margarita of Austria, wife of Felipe III. Although the handsome façade is original, architect Ventura Rodríguez remodelled the interior after a fire in the 18th century.

www.patrimonionacional.es
🕂 40B4
✉ Plaza de la Encarnación 1
☎ 91 454 8803
🕐 Tue–Sat 10:30–12:45, 4–5:45, Sun, public hols 11–1:45. Closed Fri PM, Mon and Aug
🍴 Plenty near by (€)
Ⓜ Opera
♿ None
💷 Cheap; free Wed
↔ Palacio Real (▶ 23)
❓ Joint ticket available with the nearby Monasterio de las Descalzas Reales (▶ 16)

DID YOU KNOW?

Napoleon Bonaparte put his brother, Joseph, on the throne of Spain in 1808. This precipitated the Madrid uprising against the French on the *2 de mayo* (2 May). Never accepted, José's only popular measure was the relaxation of duty on alcohol, which won him the nickname *Pepe Botella* (Joe Bottle).

MUSEO DE AMÉRICA (▶ 17, TOP TEN)

MUSEO ARQUEOLÓGICO NACIONAL ✪

The National Archaeological Museum's collection reflects
Mediterranean cultures as well as those of the Iberian
peninsula. Although the old-fashioned, glass-cased
displays could put off the younger generation, exhibits
such as the *Dama de Elche* are fascinating. Discovered
near Alicante, this finely-carved bust of a noblewoman
from Elche dates from around the 4th century BC; the hole
at the back probably held the ashes of a well-born person.
Like a photograph in *Vogue* magazine, her elaborate
headdress and jewellery reflect the fashions of Iberia, but
they also relate to Greek and Celtic styles. Moreover, they
can be traced through the centuries to the traditional hair-
styles of Valencia. Other treasures in the museum include
porcelain from the Buen Retiro factory, Greek pottery, and
an intriguing Roman sundial. In the garden, a specially dug-
out underground room contains reproductions of the
famous prehistoric cave paintings of bison and deer from
Altamira. Explanations in several languages are available.

MUSEO NACIONAL DE ANTROPOLOGÍA ✪

This would be dull were it not for the quirky objects on
display. School children rush to the ghoulish Room III, to
the left of the main entrance, to see the skeleton of the
Gigante Extremeño, Spain's tallest man. Agustín Luengo
Capilla, who died in 1849, aged 26, was an astonishing
2.35m tall. Most of the building is devoted to tribal relics:
big gods and little gods, wooden shields and dug-out
canoes. Other children's favourites include Brazilian
feathered head-dresses and gruesome shrunken heads
dangling in a glass case.

www.man.es
✚ 41F5
✉ Calle del Serrano 13
☎ 91 577 79 12/91 577 79
19/20
🕐 Tue–Sat 9:30–8:30, Sun,
public hols 9:30–2:30.
Jul–Aug Tue–Sat
9:30–6:30
🍴 Plenty near by (€)
Ⓜ Serrano, Colón
♿ Good
🎟 Cheap; free under-18,
over-65, Sat after 2:30,
Sun
↔ Calle de Serrano (▶ 34)

Above: *inside the Museo
Arqueológico Nacional*

www.mcu.es/nmuseos/
antropologia
✚ 67E1
✉ Calle Alfonso XII 68
☎ 91 530 64 18/91 539 59
95
🕐 Tue–Sat 10–7:30, Sun,
public hols 10–2
🍴 Plenty near by (€)
Ⓜ Atocha RENFE
♿ Few
🎟 Cheap (free Sat PM, Sun)

49

CALLE MAYOR

➕ 41F3
✉ Calle de Montalbán 12
☎ 91 532 64 99
🕐 Tue–Fri 9:30–3, Sat, Sun, public hols 10–3
🍴 Plenty near by (€)
Ⓜ Banco de España, Retiro
♿ Good
💰 Cheap (free for children, over 65s, and Sun)
🔄 Parque del Retiro (▶ 24)
❓ Free tour Sun 11:30 (not Jul–Sep)

MUSEO NACIONAL DE ARTES DECORATIVAS ✪✪

Like London's Victoria and Albert Museum and the Musée des Arts Decoratifs in Paris, this is a must for anyone interested in design and fine craftsmanship. Throughout the five floors of this converted mansion the collection focuses on Spanish traditions, but places them in a wider context. The glassware from La Granja, for example, contrasts with centuries-old pieces dating from Greek and Roman times as well as more modern Lalique. Porcelain from Spanish factories compares with works from elsewhere in Europe, such as Meissen, Limoges and Sèvres.

The undoubted highlight is the famous tiled kitchen on the fourth floor, brought here from a palace in Valencia. Covered in hand-painted pictorial tiles, this is a snapshot of 18th-century life that shows the mistress of the house and her retinue of servants – from the butler in frock coat and buckled shoes to the African woman wielding a broom. Food historians note the copper pots, the leg of lamb, partridge, *chorizos* (sausages) and even a tray of cakes and *turrón* (nougat) that look good enough to eat. Most fun are

the cats which are stealing a fish from the pan and an eel from the shopping basket.

Furniture, tapestries, an ornate silver tabletop showing all the signs of the zodiac – there is much to admire here. Don't, however, miss the room dedicated to the fan, that most Spanish of all fashion accessories. Follow its evolution from simple palm leaves to intricate designs in silk and mother-of-pearl. Even the language of the fan is deciphered.

MUSEO NACIONAL CENTRO DE ARTE REINA SOFÍA (► 19, TOP TEN)

MUSEO DE LA REAL ACADEMIA DE BELLAS ARTES DE SAN FERNANDO ✪✪✪

Both Picasso and Dalí studied at the grand, but grim-looking Royal Academy, the oldest museum in the city (1752). Climb the sombre, massive stone steps; once inside the gallery, all is brightly-lit. This uncrowded museum has a serendipitous charm. Although Goya's paintings are at the end of the itinerary, don't rush there

but take your time to discover Francisco Zurbarán's powerful portraits of monks, which dominate Room 6, and Rubens' *Susana y Los Viejos* (Susanna and the Elders), the highlight of Room 13. There are curiosities galore, such as Giuseppe Archimboldo's curious painting in Room 14. Called *La Primavera* (Spring), this is a portrait concocted from daisies, wild strawberries, roses and iris. Two contrasting portraits of famous generals, Napoleon Bonaparte and George Washington, dominate Room 35. The French emperor seems to be wearing a dress, while the American holds a map of the capital named after him.

Find Joaquín Sorolla (► 20) and Juan Gris among a mish-mash of modern Spanish artists in Rooms 25 and 29. Room 20 is popular for its famous but surprisingly small Goya painting, *El Entierro de la Sardina* (The Burial of the Sardine), depicting this rather bizarre local custom. Other works by Goya in the room include self-portraits, as well as sketches for the famous oils of scenes in a mad house, of the Inquisition and of penitents.

www.insde.es

🔢 41D3

✉ Calle de Alcalá 13

☎ 91 524 08 64

🕐 Tue–Fri 9–7, Sat–Mon, public hols 9–2:30 (some rooms closed from time to time)

🍴 Plenty near by (€)

Ⓜ Sevilla, Sol

♿ None

🎟 Cheap; free under-18s, over-65s, Wed

Statues adorn the Museo de Bellas Artes

The Gran Vía

CALLE MAYOR

Start in the Plaza de España.

Statues of author Miguel de Cervantes and his characters, Don Quixote and Sancho Panza, dominate the square. The two tallest structures, the Edificio España and the Torre de Madrid, were designed and built by the prolific Otamendi brothers in the early 1950s.

Walk southeast down the Gran Vía.

When Madrid expanded in the early 1900s, over 300 houses and 14 ancient streets were demolished to make way for this boulevard. New buildings, some inspired by the North American skyscraper, include 1920s–30s cinemas, such as the Capitol in the Carrión building (Gran Vía 41) and the Cine Callao (Plaza del Callao 3). The Palacio de la Prensa (Plaza del Callao 4) originally provided office workers with everything from entertainment to shops and restaurants, all under one roof.

Continue east along the Gran Vía.

At Gran Vía 28 is the Telefónica (➤ 71). This American-designed skyscraper (1929) was the tallest in the city for some 25 years. From here on, buildings are older and more heavily decorated. Note the extravagant rooftop embellishments of the 1913 Edificio del Banco Central (Gran Vía 18) and the Edificios La Estrella (Gran Vía 7 and 10). No 7 shows a Moorish influence. The walk ends at the Parisian-style Edificio Metrópolis, which is crowned by a statue of Winged Victory. Down at street level, the figure of a violet seller commemorates the street vendors whose flowers once heralded spring in the city.

Distance
1.3km

Time
3 hours including visits

Start point
Plaza de España
🚇 40B5
🚇 Plaza de España

End point
Corner of Gran Vía and Calle de Alcalá
🚇 41D4
🚇 Banco de España

Lunch
Museo del Jamón (€)
✉ Gran Vía 72
☎ 91 541 20 23

Two views of the Gran Vía

CALLE MAYOR

🔢 40A5
✉ Calle Ventura Rodríguez 17
☎ 91 547 36 46
🕐 Tue–Sat 9:30–3, Sun 10–3; Jul, Aug 10–2, Sun 10–1:30
🍴 Plenty (€)
🚇 Plaza de España, Ventura Rodríguez
♿ Few
💶 Cheap, free Wed, Sun
🔄 Iglesia de San Marcos (► 46)

MUSEO CERRALBO ⭐

The 17th Marquis of Cerralbo (1845–1922) was passionate about politics and the arts. His collection, which has to be shown as he left it, includes 30,000 'works of art, archaeological objects and curios', gathered from around the world. Although the best-known of his paintings is The *Ecstasy of St Francis of Assisi* by El Greco, there is also porcelain, Greek and Roman pottery, furniture, swords and oriental armour. Connoisseurs appreciate the aristocratic mansion as much as the artefacts. The sumptuous ballroom (renovated in 1999) contrasts with the practical office-library; even the parquet floors in the dining room and billiard room demand admiration.

DID YOU KNOW?

The ancient Burial of the Sardine ceremony painted by Goya (► 51) is still an annual event. On Ash Wednesday, a mock funeral procession – bearing a tiny coffin and accompanied by a jazz band – makes its way from the Ermita de San Antonio de la Florida (► 39) to the Los Pajaritos fountain in the Casa de Campo, where the sardine is interred.

---

www.museo-chicote.com
🔢 41D4
✉ Gran Vía 12
☎ 91 532 67 37
🕐 Mon–Sat 4PM–4AM
🚇 Gran Vía
♿ None
💶 Free
🔄 Telefónica

MUSEO CHICOTE ⭐

Not a museum, but a cocktail bar! Founded in 1931 by Perico Chicote to 'mix drinks, lives and opinions', this art deco bar survives more on memories than present-day glamour. Photos of Frank Sinatra, Salvador Dalí, Bette Davis and Ernest Hemingway line the walls, but as to who sat where and when, that depends on which waiter you ask. Chicote's museum of odd drinks and bottles has gone, but *madrileños* still come late for a cocktail, and at weekends it's the busiest museum in town – after midnight that is.

🔢 41F3
✉ Calle de Méndez Núñez 1
☎ 91 522 89 77
🕐 Tue–Sun 10–2
🍴 Plenty nearby (€)
🚇 Banco de España, Retiro
♿ Few
💶 Cheap, Sat free
🔄 Museo del Prado (► 26), Parque del Retiro (► 24)

MUSEO DEL EJÉRCITO ⭐

This imposing building, part of the former Palacio del Buen Retiro, is part of the grand expansion scheme of the Prado (► 26). For art historians, the opulent Antigua Salón de los Reinos (the throne room) holds particular significance. To add to the pomp, Velázquez was commissioned to paint 12 vast canvases celebrating battles won by Felipe IV, while Zurbarán created the 10 *Labours of Hercules*. The eccentric Army Museum that has filled the room in recent years will eventually be moved to the Alcázar in Toledo to make way for the Prado's collection of 17th-century paintings.

CALLE MAYOR

MUSEO LÁZARO GALDIANO (► 18, TOP TEN)

MUSEO NAVAL ✪

You need a working knowledge of Spanish or naval history to get the best out of this small museum. This is a pity, since Spain's maritime power changed the course of world events. In addition to numerous models of boats, there are vivid paintings depicting naval victories. A famous battle prize is the flag of the French battleship *L'Atlas* (Room VII). Napoleon presented ensigns to all his commanders before the Battle of Trafalgar in 1805 – this is the only one to survive. Don't miss Room XVII, where the routes of Spain's explorers are plotted on a world map covering an entire wall. Here, too, is the first map of the New World by a cartographer who had actually been there. Dated 1500, it was made by Juan de la Cosa, captain of the *Santa María*, one of the trio of ships led by Columbus in 1492.

MUSEO DEL PRADO (► 26, TOP TEN)

➕ 67D2
✉ Paseo del Prado 5
☎ 91 379 52 99
🕐 Tue–Sun 10–2
🍴 Plenty near by (€)
🚇 Banco de España
♿ None
🎟 Free

Above: *star parade: the bar at Museo Chicote*

55

San Gregorio Magno, *painted by Goya, in the Museo Romántico chapel*

67D4
Calle de San Mateo 13
91 448 10 45
Plenty near by (€)
Tribunal, Alonso Martínez
Closed until further notice for renovations

MUSEO ROMÁNTICO ❂

The Marqués de la Vega-Inclán (1858–1942) set up the country's tourist infrastructure and initiated the *paradores*, the national group of hotels in former castles and monasteries. His collection of 19th-century paintings, books and furniture formed the nucleus of this somewhat eccentric but entertaining museum of period ephemera (fans, old photo albums, cigar cases, duelling pistols, paintings etc), dedicated to artists and writers of a romantic bent.

MUSEO SOROLLA (► 20, TOP TEN)

MUSEO THYSSEN-BORNEMISZA (► 22, TOP TEN)

www.museodeltraje.mcu.es
66A5
Avenida Juan de Herrera 2
91 549 71 50
Mon–Sat 9:30–7, Sun and public hols 10–3
Plenty near by (€)
Moncloa, Ciudad Universitaria
Good
Cheap
Museo de América (► 17)

MUSEO DEL TRAJE ❂❂

Billed as the most up-to-date museum in Spain, the Museum of Costume opened in March 2004. The colourful collection, comprising everything from shoes to mantillas, draws on a fund of more than 21,000 items to trace the evolution of Spanish clothing and fashions from medieval times to the 20th century. The prize exhibit is the 13th-century trousseau of the Infanta María, daughter of Ferdinand III. Here you can observe the transition from the fashions of the Enlightenment, which catered exclusively for the aristocracy, to those of a more democratic, utilitarian age. The museum displays costumes designed by some of the great Spanish 20th-century couturiers, including Mariano Fortuny and Cristóbal Balenciaga, a Basque who went on to take the Parisian fashion world by storm. The museum hopes to acquire items from Queen Sophia's wardrobe from the 1960s and 70s and will feature the work of contemporary designers.

CALLE MAYOR

PALACIO DE COMUNICACIONES ✪✪

Looking like a palace on the outside and a train station within, this building could well be the world's most impressive post office. Nicknamed Nuestra Señora de las Comunicaciones, as if it were a cathedral, it dominates the Plaza de la Cibeles (➤ 62). The Banco de España stands opposite; further south, on the Paseo del Prado, is the Stock Exchange. These three grandiose buildings from the beginning of the 20th century were part of the city's programme of expansion and reflect a confidence in Madrid's future.

Inside, the post office is all marble and brass beneath a stained-glass ceiling providing plenty of natural light. The 80 different counters offer a wide variety of services from posting a parcel to paying the rent. Buying a stamp seems mundane by comparison. In the two side wings, you can stand and write your postcards at one of the 44 desks. Outside, customers slip their mail into 12 brass *buzones* (post boxes) marked Madrid, Sevilla, Valencia, Barcelona and more. There is even a special one for *urgentes*. The post office is open daily; when the main door is closed at weekends use Gate H. Within the 12,000sq m complex is a chapel for members of staff (Door Y) and the Museo Postal y de Telegráfico, at the side (Door M) on Calle de Montalbán. This has been revamped to show off one of the world's great stamp collections. The oldest stamp, from 1850, bears the face of Isabel II.

www.correos.es
🞦 41E3
✉ Plaza de la Cibeles s/n
☎ 91 521 65 00; Museum 91 396 26 79
🕓 Daily 8:30AM–9:30PM; (Museum) Mon–Fri 9–2, 5–7, Sat 9–2
🍴 Plenty near by (€)
Ⓜ Banco de España
♿ Few
🖐 Free; museum free with passport/ID
↔ Casa de América (➤ 34), Museo Naval (➤ 55), Plaza de la Cibeles (➤ 62)

The grand main post office, the Palacio de Comunicaciones

CALLE MAYOR

The home of the Spanish parliament, the Palacio de las Cortes

www.congresodelos
diputados.es

✚ 41D3

✉ Plaza de las Cortes s/n

☎ 91 390 60 00

🕐 Sat 10:30–12:45, guided tour only every 30 mins by appointment Mon–Fri. Closed Aug, public hols

🍴 Plenty near by (€)

Ⓜ Sevilla

♿ Good

💷 Cheap

↔ Museo Thyssen-Bornemisza (➤ 22)

❓ Official ID (such as a passport) required, free booklet given out

PALACIO DE LAS CORTES ✪✪

The events of 23 February 1981 marked a turning point in Spanish history. Civil Guard commander Colonel Tejero entered the *Salón de Sesiones* in the parliament building, firing his pistol and ordering delegates to the floor. Television cameras relayed the action live to a shocked country and for a while it looked as if Spain might revert to military dictatorship. Discussion of those events are the prime topic during the 45-minute tours of this neo-classical mid-19th century building. First, however, you pass through four rooms as the guide describes the ornate paintings, chandeliers and furniture. There are portraits of 19th-century politicians and an intriguing 3m-high clock that registers the weather and humidity, as well as the date and time. Spaniards study the seven constitutions of Spain – from the earliest (1812), to the current one issued in 1978 and signed by Juan Carlos.

The highlight, however, is the deputies' chamber with its 350 leather armchairs. The order of seating for the cabinet reflects the seniority of the ministry; two panels show how individual members vote: *sí, no* or *abs*. But what Spaniards of all ages want to know is, 'where are the bullet holes?' Even bored teenagers pay attention as the guide points out the 40 punctures in the walls and ceiling. Parents recall those momentous hours when tanks threatened Valencia, and Spain waited to see whether or not the new democracy would survive.

PALACIO REAL (➤ 23, TOP TEN)

PARQUE DEL RETIRO (► 24, TOP TEN)

THE PASEOS   ⭐⭐

Madrid is split down the middle, from north to south, by a series of *paseos* or boulevards: the Paseo de la Castellana (4km), the Paseo de Recoletos (1km) and the Paseo del Prado (1.5km, Walk ► 69). These are interspersed by grand roundabouts, often graced by imposing statues and fountains, such as the Plaza de la Cibeles (► 62).

Most visitors enjoy the stretch of the Paseo del Prado linking the three great art museums: the Prado (► 26), the Museo Nacional Centro de Arte Reina Sofía (► 19) and the Museo Thyssen-Bornemisza (► 22). Trees shade strollers along the eastern side of this *paseo*, which borders the Real Jardín Botánico (► 70).

The Paseo de Recoletos has echoes of Paris, with its glamorous cafés. The most famous is the Gran Café Gijón (► 99), known as a meeting place for writers and artists in the 1920s. Today, actors, agents and directors still meet to read scripts and clinch deals. In the evenings a pianist tinkles away.

The Paseo de la Castellana, which cuts through the modern part of the city, is lined with imposing office blocks and, to the north, the Estadio Santiago Bernabéu, home of Real Madrid football club (► 44). In summer, the Castellana is known for its *terrazas* (open-air cafés), which open late and close in the early hours. Locals have their favourite *terraza* where they meet to chat and drink, often to a background of music.

Botero's hand sculpture on the Paseo de la Castellana

Coffee break at the Café El Espejo on the Paseo de Recoletos

Food & Drink

Madrileños are a sociable people for whom eating and drinking in bars and restaurants is a way of life. They tend to enjoy traditional dishes made from fresh, full-flavoured ingredients, often prepared quite simply.

Tapas *come in a hundred different shapes and tastes*

Try Madrid-style cooking, then sample the cuisines from all the regions of Spain, from the Basque country to Galicia, and from Asturias to Valencia. Portions are usually hearty and prices reasonable.

In fact, the only disappointments could come when ordering non-Spanish dishes, catering for 'international' tastes.

Desserts, however, tend to be standard and unadventurous. They include the ubiquitous *flan* (crème caramel), *arroz con leche* (rice pudding) and *manzana asada* (baked apple).

Fish & Meat Dishes

Madrid is often called Spain's main fishing port because the fleets send the best of their catch straight to the city. Sauces are rarely needed for the thick slices of *lubina* (John Dory), *besugo* (sea bass) and *ventresca* (tuna), which are grilled *a la plancha* (on a hot plate). Basque restaurants are particularly well known for their fish dishes, which have relatively simple sauces, such as white wine with garlic and parsley. The Spanish are also great meat eaters, choosing between tender pork, *chuletas de lechal* (lamb chops) and chunks of *solomillo* (sirloin steak). There is also a vast array of sausages, from *chorizos* (spicy pork) to *morcilla* (black pudding).

Madrid's own dish is *cocido madrileño*, a stew of meat and vegetables that traditionally is prepared in an earthenware pot by the fire. Lamb and suckling pig are roasted slowly in wood-fired ovens, until the meat is so tender that it falls off the bone.

Snacks

Don't miss *tapas*, the little snacks that are eaten throughout the day, but especially in the late afternoon and

early evening before restaurants open for dinner. A *tapa* was once a small round slice of bread set on top of your wine glass – a simple device to stop flies crawling in! Someone added a slice of ham, an olive or a marinated pepper and – hey presto! – the *tapa* was born. An automatic companion to a small glass of wine, they range from slices of cheese or sausage to meatballs or snails. Every bar has its own speciality.

Another must is chocolate *con churros*, which are popular at breakfast or teatime. Cups of hot, thick drinking chocolate traditionally come with *churros*. Variously translated as doughnuts or fritters, these are light, crispy, deep-fried batter, shaped in Madrid-style teardrops, or in long, thick sticks, called *porras*. Dip them in sugar, or better still, dunk them in your hot chocolate.

Madrid hams (above) and wines from Chinchón and Valdepañas (below)

Wine

Spain is rich in vineyards, but in recent years there has been a renaissance in wine-making in the province of Madrid. Look for wines labelled D O Vinos de Madrid. Among the *blancos* (whites) try Albillo, Tapón de Oro and Viña Bayona. Refreshing *rosados* (rosés) are Tapón de Oro, Valfrío and Puerta del Sol, while reliable *tintos* (reds) include Valdeguerra and Tochuelo Tinto.

For those with a sweet tooth: hot chocolate and churros

41E4

The famous fountain on Plaza de la Cibeles

PLAZA DE LA CIBELES ✪

There are three spots dear to the hearts of *madrileños*: the Puerta de Alcalá arch; the statue of the bear and the *madroño* (madrona tree) in Puerto del Sol (► 64); and the Cibeles fountain in the roundabout that links the Paseo del Prado and the Paseo de Recoletos. Cybeles, the Greek goddess of fertility, sits in her chariot, which is drawn by two magnificent lions. The fountain itself was designed for Carlos III by Ventura Rodríguez in the 18th century, but these details are of little interest to Real Madrid football fans. They come here to celebrate their victories. Fans from rival Atlético de Madrid congregate at the next fountain to the south, with its statue of Neptune.

PLAZA MAYOR (► 25, TOP TEN)

PLAZA DE TOROS DE LAS VENTAS ✪✪

Whether you are for or against bullfighting, Las Ventas is an astonishing building. Dating from 1929, this is the most prestigious arena in the world – a 22,000-seat cathedral of bullfighting. A classic example of Moorish-inspired architecture, with pink brick and decorative tilework, it towers above the Las Ventas Metro stop. In the spacious forecourt, lifesize statues make convenient meeting places for friends before a *corrida* (fight). Poised in mid-air to the left of the main entrance is '*El Yiyo*' (José Cubero), while the legendary Antonio Bienvenida is carried shoulder high by admirers (to the right of the main entrance). Off to one side, a *torero* doffs his cap to Dr Fleming, the inventor of penicillin, which has saved the lives of many bullfighters. Along a wall facing the southwest side of the stadium is a mural of nine lifesize bulls and their keepers.

Fights are usually at 7 in the evening, and are said to be the only events in Spain that start right on time. Crowds gather early looking for tickets and buying nuts and sweets from stalls. The most prestigious *corridas* are during the *feria* of San Isidro, the month-long festival in May, when some 30 take place.

29C2
Calle de Alcalá 237
91 536 22 00 (stadium), 91 725 18 57 (museum); www.las-ventas.com
Bullfights: Mar–Oct; Museum: Tue–Fri 9:30–2:30, Sun 10–1; Nov–Feb Mon–Fri 9:30–2:30. Closed Mon, Sat, public hols, on day of bullfight
Plenty near by (€)
Las Ventas
Stadium few; museum none
Bullfights expensive; museum free

On the north side of the arena is the **Museo Taurino**. This small museum is a Hall of Fame for bullfighting. It traces the development of the modern style and honours the legends of the ring, who are all known by their nicknames. Portraits and busts include stars of the 19th century: 'Cúchares' (Francisco Arjona), celebrated for his innovative movements, and the rivals 'Lagartijo' (Rafael Molina) and 'Frascuelo' (Salvador Sánchez). Although words such as 'artistic' and 'elegant' describe their skills, the litany of deaths from wounds and infections is sobering. The famous 'Manolete', for example, died after being gored on 28 August 1947. The white-and-gold costume he wore that day, plus his pink cape embroidered with roses and violets, is on display next to the basic blood transfusion machine that failed to save his life. Credit is also given to the supporting *picadores* and *banderilleros* and even famous bulls: the head of the bull that killed Manuel García Espartero (1865–94) is proudly displayed.

Madrid's Plaza de Toros de Las Ventas is the world's most prestigious bullring

Man and bull are commemorated in the Museo Taurino

63

🗺 40C3
🍴 Plenty near by (€)
Ⓜ Sol
↔ Plaza Mayor (▶ 25)
❓ Crammed on New Year's Eve. Works around the metro station for the foreseeable future

The Puerta del Sol marks the crossroads of the city

PUERTA DEL SOL ✪✪

Streets radiate in all directions from this oblong plaza, literally the Gateway to the Sun and one of the focal points of Madrid. Dominating all he surveys is Carlos III (1759–88) astride a horse and usually with a pigeon perched on his royal head. The words on the plinth are a paean of praise to the king, who is regarded as 'the best mayor of Madrid'. He looks across at the handsome Casa de Correos, the post office from 1766–1847. To the right of the main entrance, a plaque honours the heroes of the *2 de mayo*, the rebellion on 2 May 1808 against the French army that had occupied the capital. Set in the pavement in front of the Casa de Correos, another plaque marks Kilometre 0, the *Origen de las Carreteras Radiales*. This is the point from which all distances to and from Madrid are measured. Other statues in this busy square include *La Mariblanca*, next to the station, and the emblem of Madrid – the famous *oso* (bear) standing on his hind legs and eating fruit from the *madroño* (madrona tree). Find it behind the Carlos III statue.

🗺 40B1

PUERTA DE TOLEDO ✪✪

How are the mighty fallen! In 1808, when Frenchman Joseph Bonaparte was installed as king of Spain by his brother Napoleon, he gave orders for a triumphal arch to be erected at the Toledo gate. After Joseph was ousted by Fernando VII in 1814, work continued on the arch, but the triumph it celebrated was the Spanish defeat of the French! Another triumphal arch, the Puerta de Alcalá, is also lost in traffic, at the northwest corner of the Parque del Retiro. A symbol of Madrid, this is best appreciated at night, when it is tastefully floodlit.

EL RASTRO
(RASTRO FLEA MARKET)

✪✪✪

Sunday would not be Sunday without a visit to the Rastro Flea Market. This sprawl of stalls attracts as many locals as visitors, even if they have no intention of buying anything. Start at the Plaza de Cascorro, with its statue of El Cascorro (Eloy Gonzalo), a 19th-century hero of the Spanish-American war in Cuba. The stalls here sell leather bags, weird crafts and perfumes of dubious origin. Once you reach the trees that shade Calle de la Ribera de Curtidores, the quality improves, with shops making solid furniture and wrought-iron weather vanes. Bars and pastry shops along the street are also open. In a courtyard, through an ancient arch, is the Galerías Piquer, a complex of 50 antiques shops selling everything from clocks to oriental furniture.

Explore side streets such as Calle de San Cayetano, Calle de Rodas and Calle de Fray Ceferino González, for art equipment and picture frames, bird cages and fishing nets.

🔲 40C1
✉ Calle de Ribera de Curtidores
🕐 Sun, public hols AM
🍴 Plenty near by (€)
🚇 La Latina, Puerta de Toledo
🚌 Puerta de Toledo (➤ 64)

DID YOU KNOW?

The Casa de Correos clock is an integral part of Spain's New Year celebrations. As it strikes midnight, Spaniards all over the country watch television and eat *las uvas de la suerte* (lucky grapes), gulping down one grape per chime to ensure their good fortune in the new year.

Sunday fun at the Rastro flea market

CALLE MAYOR

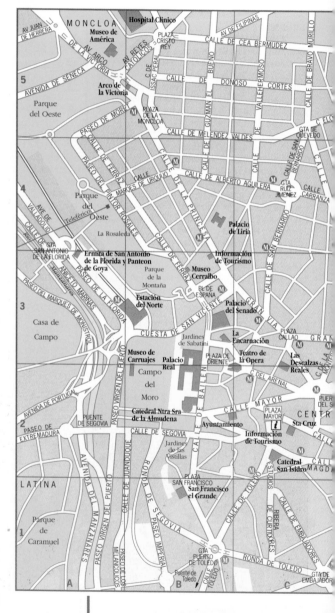

CALLE MAYOR

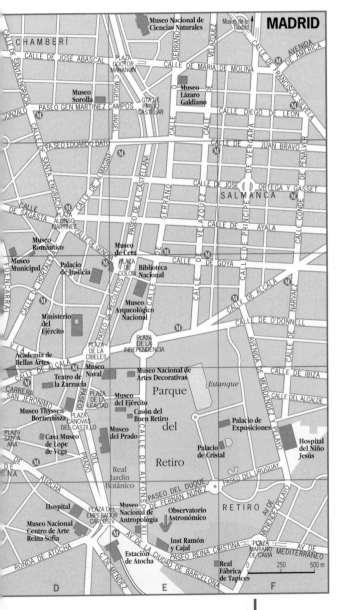

MADRID

CHAMBERÍ

CALLE DE SANTA ENGRACIA

CALLE DE JOSÉ ABASCAL

PLAZA DOCTOR MARAÑON

CALLE DE MARÍA DE MOLINA

Museo Nacional de Ciencias Naturales

Museo de la Ciudad

SERRANO

VELAZQUEZ

CALLE DE FRANCISCO SILVELA

AVENIDA DE AMERICA

GONZALO

PASEO GEN MARTINEZ CAMPOS

Museo Sorolla

C. MIGUEL ANGEL

GTA DE EMILIO CASTELAR

Museo Lázaro Galdiano

CALLE DIEGO DE LEON

CALLE DE JUAN BRAVO

DE PEÑALVER

CALLE DE SANTA ENGRACIA

PASEO EDUARDO DATO

CALLE DE ALMAGRO

PASEO DE LA CASTELLANA

CALLE DE VERGARA

CALLE DE JOSE ORTEGA Y GASSET

SALAMANCA

DE CONDE

CALLE DE SAGASTA

PLAZA ALONSO MARTINEZ

CALLE DE GENOVA

SERRANO

VELAZQUEZ

CALLE DE PRINCIPE

CALLE DE AYALA

Museo Romántico

CALLE DE HORTALEZA

Museo de Cera

CALLE DE

CALLE DE GOYA

NARVAEZ

Museo Municipal

CALLE FUENCARRAL

Palacio de Justicia

PLAZA DE COLON

Biblioteca Nacional

CALLE DE ALCALÁ

Ministerio del Ejército

PASEO DE RECOLETOS

Museo Arqueológico Nacional

CALLE DE O'DONNELL

Academia de Bellas Artes

PLAZA DE LA CIBELES

PLAZA DE LA INDEPENDENCIA

AVENIDA DE MENDEZ Y PELAYO

GRAN VIA

CALLE DE ALCALÁ

Museo Naval

Museo Nacional de Artes Decorativas

CALLE DE IBIZA

Teatro de la Zarzuela

PLAZA DE LA LEALTAD

Parque

Estanque

CALLE DEL ALCALDE

CARRERA SAN JERONIMO

Museo del Ejército

Museo Thyssen-Bornemisza

PLAZA CANOVAS DEL CASTILLO

Casón del Buen Retiro

del

Palacio de Exposiciones

Hospital del Niño Jesús

PLAZA SANTA ANA

Casa Museo de Lope de Vega

Museo del Prado

Retiro

Palacio de Cristal

PASEO DEL URUGUAY

ATOCHA

PASEO DEL PRADO

Real Jardín Botánico

CALLE DE ALFONSO XII

PASEO DEL DUQUE DE FERNAN NUÑEZ

RETIRO

AV DE MENDEZ Y PELAYO

Hospital

PLAZA DEL EMPERADOR CARLOS V

Museo Nacional de Antropología

Observatorio Astronómico

PLAZA MARIANO DE CAVIA

AV DE MEDITERRANEO

Museo Nacional Centro de Arte Reina Sofía

AV DE LA CIUDAD DE BARCELONA

Inst Ramón y Cajal

PASEO REINA CRISTINA

RONDA DE ATOCHA

C. DE MENDEZ

Estación de Atocha

Real Fábrica de Tapices

0   250   500 m

D   E   F

The Paseo del Prado

Distance
1.5km

Time
One day, including visits

Start point
Estación de Atocha
 41E1
Ⓜ Estación de Atocha

End point
Plaza de la Cibeles
🚏 41E4
Ⓜ Banco de España

Tea
Hotel Ritz (€€)
✉ Plaza de la Lealtad 5
☎ 91 521 28 57

Start at the Atocha Railway Station.

The 19th-century station has been converted into an astonishing botanic garden; the high-speed trains leave from the hi-tech station annexe. Across the street is the Museo Nacional Centro de Arte Reina Sofía (➤ 19).

Walk north along the Paseo del Prado.

This is the southern end of a chain of boulevards passing several major attractions (➤ 59). Walk along the east side of the street, past the Real Jardín Botánico (➤ 70) and the Prado (➤ 26). On the left, in the Plaza de Cánovas del Castillo, is a fountain with a statue of Neptune. Beyond that is the Museo Thyssen-Bornemisza (➤ 22), the third of Madrid's spectacular art galleries.

The Puerta de Alcalá was built by Carlos III in the mid-18th century as a grand entrance to the city

Continue north on the Paseo del Prado.

Walk past the Hotel Ritz (Lealtad 5; ► 13, 102), and the railings on the Plaza de la Lealtad, which enclose an obelisk dedicated to the local heroes who died on 2 May 1808 in the revolt against the French. The next grand façade on the right (Lealtad 11) is the Bolsa, the Madrid Stock Exchange. Once past the Museo Naval (► 55), you reach the Plaza de la Cibeles (► 62), with its fountain. The grandiose building on the right is the Palacio de Comunicaciones (► 57), perhaps the most glamorous post office in the world. Off to the right, on the Calle de Alcalá, is the Puerta de Alcalá. This monumental arch, built by Carlos III, is considered the symbol of Madrid.

The Neptune fountain on the Plaza de Canovas del Castillo

www.realfatapices.com
🔲 67F1
✉ Calle de Fuenterrabía 2
☎ 91 434 05 50
🕐 Mon–Fri 10–2. Closed Aug
🍴 Plenty near by (€)
🚇 Atocha RENFE, Menendez Pelayo
♿ None 🎟 Cheap
🔁 Museo Nacional de Antropología (➤ 49)
❓ All visits in small guided groups

Above: *running repairs at the Real Fábrica de Tapices*

🔲 41F2
✉ Plaza de Murillo 2
☎ 91 420 30 17
🕐 10–sunset
🍴 Plenty near by (€)
🚇 Atocha
♿ None
🎟 Cheap; over 65s and children under 10 free
🔁 Museo del Prado (➤ 26)

Opposite: *ride the Teleférico for great views over the city*
70

REAL FÁBRICA DE TAPICES ⭐⭐

Not a museum, this factory hums with the sounds of men and women making and repairing carpets and tapestries. The methods have changed little, if at all, over the centuries since the van der Goten family were brought here from Flanders in the 18th century by Felipe V. The 200-year-old looms are still anchored by massive tree trunks to keep the tapestry taut, and woollen threads are still spun by hand, carefully mixed with silk to create some 3,000 subtly different shades.

Many of the tapestries are still based on cartoons by the famous Spanish painters of the day, including Goya (➤ 14). The time and effort required to complete a tapestry is astonishing: one square metre takes five months and costs over €9,000. Visitors tend to 'ooh' and 'aah' as they stare at workers who are using medieval skills in a medieval setting.

REAL JARDÍN BOTÁNICO ⭐⭐

On a hot summer day there is nowhere better to stroll or snooze on a bench than these royal botanic gardens. In celebration of its bicentenary (1981), the geometric gardens were renovated and remodelled; today there are three terraced areas to explore. Closest to the Paseo del Prado are 14 plots devoted to plants and herbs used for cooking, medicines and decoration. Some are indigenous to Spain and Portugal. In the late afternoon, enjoy the heady scent of the aromatics in plot 11. Dotted with fountains, the middle terrace is a living encyclopaedia of plants – from the oldest known to man to the most highly developed species – all arranged in the correct scientific order. Appropriately, a bust of Linnaeus, the Swedish botanist who invented this classification system for plants, overlooks the gardens. Like Kew Gardens in England, the Jardín Botánico is also a scientific institution, with a seed bank of plants from around the world as well as the Iberian Peninsula.

CALLE MAYOR

TELEFÉRICO ✪✪

The most spectacular views of the Madrid skyline are from the Teleférico cable-car. Since 1969 it has glided from the Paseo del Pintor Rosales, just north of the Plaza de España, across to the scrubby parkland of the Casa de Campo. On board, a taped, but muffled, Spanish commentary points out landmarks as you swing across the newly planted gardens of the Parque del Oeste, the twin domes of the Ermita de San Antonio de la Florida (➤ 39) and the Río Manzanares. The 11-minute, 2.5km ride terminates in a modern block with a very ordinary cafeteria and snack bar.

🔢 66A4
✉ Paseo del Pintor Rosales s/n
☎ 91 541 74 50
🕐 Apr to mid-Sep daily 12–8; mid-Sep to Mar, Sat, Sun & hols 12–6
🍴 Restaurant/café (€)
Ⓜ Argüelles
♿ None 🚻 Moderate
↔ Ermita de San Antonio de la Florida (➤ 39)

TELEFÓNICA ✪

One of the city's first skyscrapers, the Telefónica was designed by American architect Lewis Weeks. Opened in 1929 as the headquarters of Spain's national telephone service, it symbolised the country's move into the modern era. A few years later, Franco's gunners used its 81m height as a gauge for shelling the Gran Vía during the Siege of Madrid. Take time to see the telephone company's collection of paintings and sculptures by Spanish artists such as Picasso, Chillida, Gris and Tapiès. Enter via the side door at Calle de Fuencarral 3.

🔢 41D4
✉ Fuencarral 3
☎ 91 522 66 45 (gallery)
🕐 Tue–Fri 10–2, 5–8; Sat, Sun, public hols 10–2
🍴 Plenty near by (€)
Ⓜ Gran Vía
♿ Few
🚻 Free with passport
↔ Museo Chicote (➤ 54)

71

Calle de Alcalá

Distance
1.2km

Time
Half a day including visits

Start point
Banco de España
✚ 41E3
🔲 Banco de España

End point
Teatro Real
✚ 40B3
🔲 Opéra

Lunch/snack
Círculo de Bellas Artes (€)
✉ Calle del Marqués de
   Casa Riera 2
☎ 91 531 85 03

Start at the Banco de España Metro station and walk west.

The Calle de Alcalá runs east towards the university town of Alcalá de Henares. On the north side, where it converges with the Gran Vía, is the 19th-century Iglesia de San José, popular with South Americans who want to see where early 19th-century revolutionary hero, Simón Bolívar was married. Opposite is the elaborate 1926 Círculo de Bellas Artes (No 42), an arts club with a café and outdoor terrace. Anyone can pay a small fee for day membership, then relax over coffee or a drink.

Cross over and continue on the north side of the Calle de Alcalá.

At No 25 is the Iglesia de las Calatravas (➤ 45), a church with an ornate façade. A few doors down is the Casino de Madrid (No 15), a private gentleman's club, not a gambling casino. No 13 is the Museo de la Real Academia de Bellas Artes de San Fernando (➤ 51) and No 3 is the massive Ministry of Finance, which was built as the Customs House in the 18th century. The next square is the busy Puerta del Sol (➤ 64).

Carry on across the square to the Calle del Arenal with its busy shops and restaurants.

Right: *one of Madrid's most popular landmarks – the bear and* madroña *tree in the Puerta del Sol*

Below: *The refurbished Teatro Real now has one of the best auditoriums in Europe*

The first church on the left is San Ginés, with a painting by El Greco in an adjacent chapel. The walk ends at the Plaza Isabel II, which is dominated by the Teatro Real.

In the Know

If you only have a short time to visit Madrid, or would like to get a real flavour of the city, here are some ideas:

Ways to Be a Local

Stop for a siesta – and enjoy the nightlife.

Cool off in the afternoon in a cinema on the Gran Vía (➤ 53).

Order a *horchata de chufa* – a traditional cold summer drink made from the *chufa* nut.

Play chess in the Parque del Retiro (➤ 24) on Sunday morning.

Go to a *zarzuela* (light opera) performance.

Drink hot chocolate with *churros* at dawn in the Chocolatería San Ginés (➤ 99).

Buy biscuits from the Convento de las Carboneras (➤ 38).

Watch the sunset by the Templo de Debod, below the Plaza de España.

Order a *cocido madrileño* (traditional stew) at La Posada de la Villa (➤ 95).

Don't look like a tourist by wearing shorts and halter-tops; think smart casual.

Good Places to Have Lunch

Angel (€)
✉ Augusto Figueroa 35 ☎ 91 521 70 12. Near the Gran Vía but away from the tourists, this tiny, atmospheric bistro is ideal for an intimate lunch.

Brasserie de Lista (€)
✉ Serrano 10 ☎ 91 411 0864. In Madrid's poshest shopping district. Sit outside under the parasols and count the carrier bags with designer labels passing by.

El Espejo (€)
✉ Paseo de Recoletos 31 ☎ 91 308 23 47. Here you can linger over a coffee or beer and *tapas* on the outdoor terrace of this pavilion overlooking

Enjoying a coffee at Bar Castellano on Paseo de la Castellana

Paseo de Recoletos (➤ 59).

A' Casiña (€–€€)
✉ Avenida del Angel s/n ☎ 91 526 34 25. Located in the Casa de Campo, so lunching here is like eating out in the country.

Casa Labra (€)
✉ Calle de Tuetuán 12 ☎ 91 513 00 81. Eat cod at the birthplace of the Spanish Socialist Party.

Casa Mingo (€)
✉ Glorieta de San Antonio de la Florida 2 ☎ 91 547 79 18. After seeing the Goya ceiling next door, everyone comes here for roast chicken, sausages and cider – plain, simple and cheap.

Gran Café Gijón (€)
✉ Paseo de Recoletos 21 ☎ 91 521 54 25. Order the menu of the day for a bargain lunch in plush art nouveau surroundings.

Hotel Ritz (€€–€€€)
✉ Plaza de la Lealtad 5
☎ 91 701 67 67. The shady garden, scented by flowers, is a delightful spot for Sunday brunch. Expensive but worth it.

Museo Thyssen-Bornemisza (€)
✉ Paseo del Prado 8
☎ 91 369 01 51. Sit at the bar or at a table for modern food in a stylish setting, in the basement of the museum.

La Posada de la Villa (€)
✉ Calle de la Cava Baja 9
☎ 91 366 18 60. When exploring the old city, stop in this medieval tavern for a taste of some traditional, hearty dishes.

Great Views

From the glass elevators on the outside of the Museo Nacional Centro de Arte Reina Sofía (➤ 19)

From the top of Faro de Madrid, Avenida de los Reyes Católicos
☎ 91 544 81 04

From the swimming pool at the top of the Hotel Emperador, Gran Vía 53,
☎ 91 547 28 00

From a cable-car on the Teleférico (➤ 71)

From a café in the Jardines de las Vistillas

Private Art Galleries

Major companies have invested in modern art collections that are open to the public during office hours:
• Fundación Mapre Vida, Avenida General Perón 40
  ☎ 91 581 16 28
• Fundación Carlos de Amberes, Calle Clandio Coello 99
  ☎ 91435 22 01

The Faro de Madrid offers a 360° panoramic view

• Fundación La Caixa, Calle Serrano 60 ☎ 91 426 0202
• Fundación Juan March, Calle de Castelló 77
  ☎ 91 435 42 40
• Fundación Telefónica, Fuencarral 3 (➤ 71)
  ☎ 91 584 2300

Best *Terrazas*

Most open at 10PM and close in the early hours.
• **El Balcón de Rosales**, Paseo del Pintor Rosales/ Marqués de Urquijo
• **Bolero**, Paseo de la Castellana 33
• **Café de Oriente**, Plaza de Orient 2
• **El Jardín de las Delicias**, Paseo de Cristino Martos 5
• **La Vieja Estación**, behind Atocha Railway Station

Things to Do on Sunday Morning

• Walk in the Retiro (➤ 24).
• See the stamp dealers in the Plaza Mayor (➤ 25).
• See the *Taller Abierto* (open studio) paintings in the Plaza del Conde de Barajas.
• Go to the Rastro Flea Market (➤ 65).
• Beat the crowds at the Museo Nacional Centro de Arte Reina Sofía and the Prado. Free all day Sun (➤ 19, 26).

Plaza Mayor

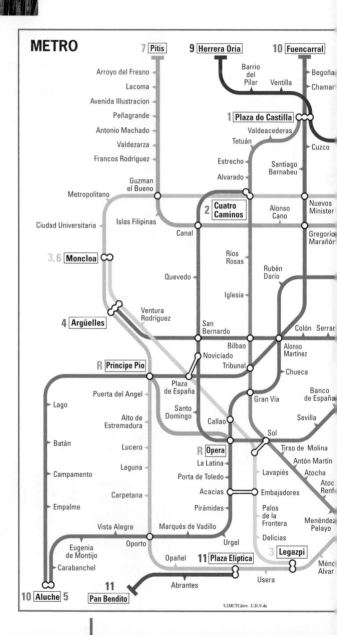

METRO

7 Pitís 9 Herrera Oria 10 Fuencarral

Arroyo del Fresno
Lacoma
Avenida Illustración
Peñagrande
Antonio Machado
Valdezarza
Francos Rodríguez
Guzman el Bueno
Metropolitano
Ciudad Universitaria
Islas Filipinas
Canal

3, 6 Moncloa

4 Argüelles

Ventura Rodríguez

R Principe Pio

Puerta del Angel
Lago
Alto de Estremadura
Batán
Lucero
Campamento
Laguna
Empalme
Carpetana
Vista Alegre
Eugenia de Montijo
Carabanchel
Oporto

10 Aluche 5

11 Pan Bendito

Barrio del Pilar Ventilla Begoña
Chamar

1 Plaza do Castilla

Valdeacederas
Tetuán
Estrecho
Alvarado

2 Cuatro Caminos

Ríos Rosas
Quevedo
Iglesia

San Bernardo
Noviciado
Tribunal

Plaza de España
Santo Domingo
Callao

R Opera
La Latina
Porta de Toledo
Acacias
Pirámides
Marqués de Vadillo
Opañel

11 Plaza Elíptica

Abrantes

Cuzco
Santiago Bernabeu

Alonso Cano

Nuevos Minister

Gregorio Marañón

Rubén Darío

Colón Serrar

Bilbao Alonso Martínez

Chueca

Gran Vía Banco de España

Sevilla

Sol

Tirso de Molina
Antón Martín
Lavapiés Atocha
Atoc Renf
Embajadores
Palos de la Frontera Menéndez Pelayo
Delicias

3 Legazpi

Urgel
Usera Ménc Alvar

V.2MCTCderv. U.D.N.4a

76

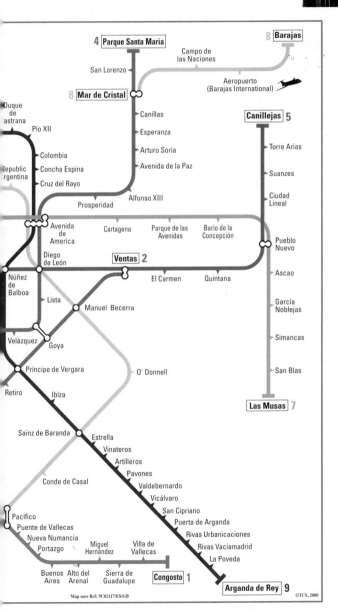

4 | Parque Santa María

Campo de las Naciones

San Lorenzo

8 | Barajas

Aeropuerto (Barajas International)

8 | Mar de Cristal

Duque de Pastrana

Pío XII

Canillas

Esperanza

Arturo Soria

Avenida de la Paz

Canillejas | **5**

Colombia

Concha Espina

Cruz del Rayo

Republic Argentina

Prosperidad

Alfonso XIII

Torre Arias

Suanzes

Ciudad Lineal

Avenida de America

Cartagena

Parque de las Avenidas

Bario de la Concepción

Diego de León

Ventas | **2**

El Carmen

Quintana

Pueblo Nuevo

Núñez de Balboa

Lista

Manuel Becerra

Ascao

García Noblejas

Velázquez

Goya

Príncipe de Vergara

O' Donnell

Simancas

San Blas

Retiro

Ibíza

Las Musas | **7**

Sainz de Baranda

Estrella

Vinateros

Artilleros

Pavones

Conde de Casal

Valdebernardo

Vicálvaro

San Cipriano

Puerta de Arganda

Rivas Urbanicaciones

Rivas Vaciamadrid

La Poveda

Pacífico

Puente de Vallecas

Nueva Numancia

Portazgo

Miguel Hernández

Villa de Vallecas

Buenos Aires

Alto del Arenal

Sierra de Guadalupe

Congosto | **1**

Arganda de Rey | **9**

Excursions from the City

Within a short drive or train ride from Madrid are some of the finest medieval towns in Europe. Toledo is not only the city of El Greco, but once boasted three distinct cultures; the pride of Alcalá de Henares was its great university; Segovia is dominated by a magnificent Roman aqueduct; and the jewel of Aranjuez is its royal palace. Since these towns are crowded with visitors during the holiday season, their rich blends of art and architecture, alleyways and hidden squares are best enjoyed in the evening or in the early morning. Consider staying overnight.

Also within the *comunidad* (autonomous community) of Madrid are the Sierra de Guadarrama to the north of the city. Dotted with small towns and villages, the mountains offer cool relief in summer, while in winter they are a popular destination for skiers.

> '*This imperial gesture…still strode across the valley with massive grace, a hundred vistas framed by its soaring arches…stepping like a mammoth among the houses…*'
>
> LAURIE LEE
> *As I Walked out one Midsummer's Morning* (1969)
> (on the aqueduct at Segovia)

ALCALÁ DE HENARES ★★

In 1998, UNESCO recognised Alcalá de Henares as the first town designed and built exclusively as a university town. About 30km due east of Madrid, the Universidad Complutense was founded in 1498, and was soon one of Europe's great seats of learning. In the past 25 years, the area around the Plaza de Cervantes, the heart of the old town, has been successfully restored. What were *colegios* (or student halls of residence) have been converted into schools, hotels and restaurants, but the ornate Renaissance façade of the **Colegio Mayor de San Ildefonso** (University of Alcalá de Henares) gives some idea of the original grandeur of the university headquarters. This administered 40 colleges and 10,000 students. Inside were three *patios* or courtyards. The third, El Trilingüe (1557), was where students from the schools of Hebrew, Greek and Latin would meet to chat in three languages. The Paraninfo (Great Hall) is still used for solemn university ceremonies, while the 15th-century chapel of San Ildefonso holds a richly-sculpted marble memorial to the hugely influential Catholic leader, Cardinal Cisneros, the founder of the university.

Alcalá de Henares was also the birthplace of Miguel de Cervantes Saavedra (1547–1616), author of the international favourite, *El Quijote* (or *Don Quixote*). At No 48 on the attractive Calle Mayor main street is the **Casa Natal de Cervantes**. This is a reproduction of the writer's alleged birthplace, with an interior *patio* typical of the 16th century, and appropriate furniture for the era. Be sure to take home the local delicacy: *almendras garrapiñadas* (caramel covered almonds).

81E3

Cervantes Train: weekends mid-Apr to Jun, Sep–1st week Dec, leaves Atocha Madrid 11AM, departs Alcalá 7PM

Callejón Santa María 2
☎ 91 881 06 34
🕐 Jul–Aug, 10–2, 5–7; Sep–Jun 10–2, 4–6:30

Colegio Mayor de San Ildefonso

✉ Plaza de San Diego
☎ 91 885 40 00
🕐 Mon–Fri guided tours 11:30, 12:30, 1:30, 4:30, 5:30; Sat, Sun 11, 11:45, 12:30,1:15, 2, 4, 4:45, 5:30, 6:15, 7
💰 Cheap

Casa Natal de Cervantes

✉ Calle Mayor 48
☎ 91 889 96 54
🕐 Mon–Fri 10:15–1:40, 4–6:30; Sat, Sun 10:15–1:30, 4–6:15
💰 Free

The university at Alcalá de Henares was reborn in the 1970s

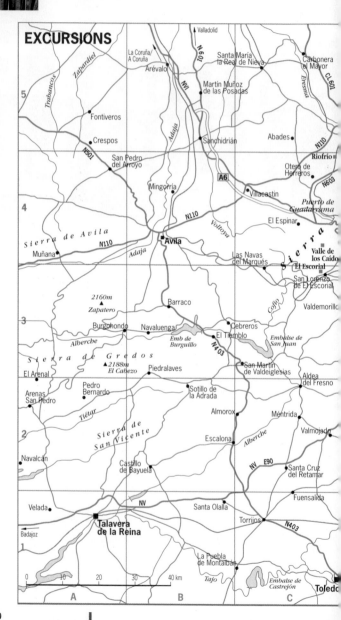

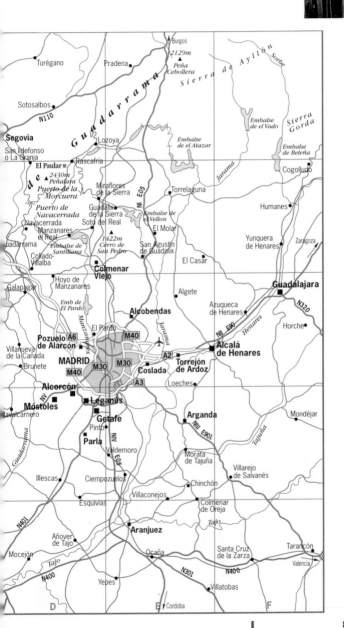

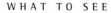

www.aranjuez.net

🔲 81E1

🚆 *Tren de la Fresa*, Atocha,
Madrid weekends 10AM
Apr–Oct (not Aug)
☎ 90 222 88 22

🍴 Plenty near by (€)

ℹ Plaza de San Antonio
☎ 91 891 04 27
🕐 Tue–Sun 10–2, 4–6
(summer); 10–1, 3–5
(winter)

❓ 35-min tour on tourist
trolley. Hourly from
tourist office, from 10AM
(not Mon, public hols)
☎ 925 14 22 74

**Palacio Real, Casa del
Labrador**
☎ 91 891 13 44
🕐 Tue–Sun 10–6:15
(Apr–Sep); 10–5:15
(Oct–Mar)
👐 Cheap, Wed free EU
citizens
❓ Main floor closed for
restoration

*The Real Capilla de San
Antonio (Royal Chapel),
Aranjuez*

ARANJUEZ ⭐⭐⭐

Thanks to the haunting theme of the *Concierto de Aranjuez* by Joaquín Rodrigo, music-lovers around the world know the name of this town. Just 50km south of Madrid, Aranjuez became a royal retreat 300 years ago. Today it is a popular destination for *madrileños*, who come for a day out, particularly in early summer when the asparagus and *fresones* (large local strawberries) are in season. They stroll along tree-lined boulevards and through the gardens, take a boat ride on the Río Tajo (River Tagus) and tour the **Palacio Real**. This enormous baroque palace was built in the early 18th century for Felipe V. Although the façade and the interior remain much as they were, two wings were added later. Inside are paintings and frescoes and, best of all, the Sala de las Porcelanas. The porcelain tiles, made in Madrid, portray scenes from Chinese life, as well as children's games.

Heading east from the palace, follow the Calle de la Reina to the 150ha Jardín del Príncipe and, further along, the **Casa del Labrador**. Whimsically named the Worker's Cottage, it is opulently decorated and full of treasures, such as the Gabinete de Platino, with idazzling inlays of platinum, gold and bronze. Aranjuez is at its loveliest in March and April when the gardens are in bloom, but is most fun in May during the festivities for San Fernando (30 May) and in September, during the Fiestas del Motín. On weekends between April and October take the *Tren de la Fresa* (Strawberry Train) with its wooden carriages, steam engine and costumed hostesses distributing strawberries.

Old Towns South of Madrid

This route south includes three historic towns: one ancient, one royal and one a fortress.

Leave Madrid on the M-30/E-901, then take the A-3 for Chinchón. Before the main exit to Arganda, take the turning for Chinchón, the M-311. Take the left turn for Morata de Tajuña, with its view over the valley. Once on flat ground, you pass Anís de Chinchón, the distillery of the popular aniseed-flavoured drink. Then it's up to the opposite ridge, and down into the next valley, where Chinchón stands high on a hillside.

Distance
200km

Time
9 hours with stops, 5 hours without stops

Start/end point
Madrid
✚ 81E3

Lunch
La Perdiz (€–€€)
✉ Calle de los Reyes
Católicos 7, Toledo
☎ 925 21 46 58

Head for the Plaza Mayor, a perfect film set for a costume drama in medieval Spain. Surrounded by rows of balconied houses, it is a ready-made arena, where bullfights and theatrical performances are still held. Have lunch at one of the many restaurants with tables outdoors. A former convent has been converted into a stylish *parador*. Parking is difficult in town, so leave the car on the outskirts and walk into the centre.

From Chinchón, take the M-305 for Aranjuez.

Chinchón retains medieval memories

Villaconejos, known for its melons, is a typical blend of old and new, the attractive and bland. Carry on to the royal town of Aranjuez (➤ 82).

From Aranjuez, take the N-400 for Ocaña and Toledo.

You can see Toledo's castle from afar, standing guard over the plain below. Park in one of the car parks at the foot of the hill and explore this walled city on foot (➤ 88).

Return to Madrid on the N-401 motorway.

☎ 91 890 59 02

🕐 Tue–Sun 10–6 (summer); 10–5 (winter)

🍴 Plenty near by (€)

ℹ ☎ 91 890 53 13

♿ Few

Ⓜ Moderate

❓ Regular foreign language guided tours from Calle Floridablanca 10

Valle de los Caídos

✚ 80C4

☎ 91 890 56 11

🕐 Tue–Sun 10–6 (summer); 10–5 (winter)

🚌 From El Escorial Tue–Sun 3:15

♿ Few

Ⓜ Moderate

Above: *the vast and rather forbidding façade of El Escorial monastery*

✚ 81D4

🍴 Café and picnic spots

❓ Restrictions of number of cars admitted to La Pedriza car park

EL ESCORIAL ✪✪✪

The first impression of the Real Monasterio de San Lorenzo de El Escorial is always its vast size. Some 50km northwest of Madrid, this combination of monastery, palace and royal mausoleum was built to celebrate victory against the French in the battle of St Quentin in 1557. Six years later, Felipe II set out to flaunt Spain's roles as rulers of the world and as the bulwark of Roman Catholicism against the forces of the Reformation. It took only 21 years to complete and has 1,200 doors, 2,600 windows and some 24km of corridors. The result must have impressed both the king's subjects and his European rivals.

The interior, including the royal apartments, is surprisingly austere, reflecting Felipe II's taste. Highlights include the Nuevos Museos (New Museum of Art), with major works by Titian, Tintoretto, Veronese, Rubens and van Dyck. Among several fine paintings by El Greco are *The Martyrdom of St Maurice* (one of his finest, though Felipe II did not like it) and *The Dream of Felipe II*, portraying the ascetic king at prayer in paradise. The heart of El Escorial is the vast basilica, which is reminiscent of St Peter's in Rome, while the library (one of Felipe II's pet projects) holds an important collection of 15th- and 16th-century books. With its lavish baroque decoration, the pantheon is the burial place of the Spanish royal family. Carlos I was the first to be buried there. Expect crowds at weekends.

Marked by a 150m high cross, the **Valle de los Caídos** (Valley of the Fallen), 9km north, is a monument to General Franco and the Falangists (the Spanish Fascists).

MANZANARES EL REAL ✪

In summer, *madrileños* head for the cooler heights of the Sierra de Guadarrama and the town of Manzanares El Real, 47km north of the capital. Legend has it that Felipe II considered establishing El Escorial (► above) here.

Left: *the grandiose library at El Escorial holds 40,000 books, plus precious manuscripts and codices*

Above: *flag flying on one of the turrets of Manzanares castle*

Certainly the 15th-century castle, with its backdrop of the Sierra de Pedriza, is dramatic. Built for the dukes of Infantado, the fortress retains Moorish features such as honeycomb cornices. Explore the quiet gardens bordering the banks of the Río Manzanares, then head for the open spaces of La Pedriza Regional Park, highly prized for its invigorating mountain air, nature trails, panoramic views, wildlife (Griffin vultures) and the oddly shaped granite boulders littering the hillsides.

EL PARDO ✪

Like the Valle de los Caídos (➤ 84), El Pardo has uncomfortable associations with the recent past, as the Palacio del Pardo was General Franco's main residence for some 35 years. However, before that, the village was a royal favourite for centuries. Felipe II and Carlos III came to hunt, and added to the comforts of the elegant 16th-century palace, which is now used to entertain foreign heads of state. (The present royal family lives just 5km away at the Zarzuela Palace).

Although part of the palace is open, the public rarely comes in numbers. However, the 200 Flemish and Spanish tapestries, as well as paintings by Spanish masters, are of interest.

🚩 81D3
✉ Paseo del Pardo
☎ 91 376 15 68
🕐 Mon–Sat 10:30–6, Sun, public hols 9:25–1:40 (summer); 10:30–5, Sun, public hols 9:55–1:40 (winter). Closed occasionally for official functions
🍴 Plenty near by (€)
✋ Cheap; free Wed for EU citizens

Segovia's magnificent Roman aqueduct still looms over the city

www.segoviaturismo.com

🔲 81D5

🍴 Plenty (€)

ℹ Plaza del Azoguejo
  ☎ 921 46 60 70
  🕐 10–8; Plaza Mayor 10

❓ Free guided tours of Segovia start here, Jul–Sep 10, 11, 12 (inner city), 4:30 (outer city)

❓ 40-minute tour on tourist trolley. Mon–Thu, Sun runs on the hour 11–1, 4–6, Fri, Sat 11–1, 4–11
  ☎ 925 14 22 74

El Alcázar

✉ Plaza de la Reina Victoria Eugenia

☎ 921 46 07 59

🕐 10–7 (summer); 10–6 (winter)

♿ Few

💲 Cheap

SEGOVIA ●●●

The old city of Segovia is surprisingly intact and unspoiled by 20th-century buildings. Standing between the Río Eresma and the Arroyo Clamores, with the Sierra de Guadarrama as a backdrop, the city's strategic importance explains its long history.

Segovia is best known for its Roman aqueduct. You can't miss the two tiers of 163 arches built of precisely cut granite, without mortar. Standing 29m above the ground at its highest point, it stretches for 813m; the water that once flowed along the channel started its journey some 15km away. This is an awesome piece of civil engineering; by comparison, the brick-and-mortar city wall looks positively messy.

Pick up a map at the tourist information office on Plaza del Azoguejo and head off to explore the old streets. Follow Calle de Cervantes, where the façade of the Casa de los Picos looks like a studded shield. This delightful street of half-timbered houses with wrought-iron balconies changes name as it winds its way uphill; perhaps that is why locals just call it the Calle Real. At the top are the Plaza Mayor and the 16th-century cathedral. Further along the Calle Real is El Alcázar. Looking like Sleeping Beauty's castle, complete with turrets and towers, it stands on top of sheer cliffs, with commanding views across the plain below. Late on Friday and Saturday nights, the city's ancient monuments are illuminated. No visit is complete without sampling the slow-cooked lamb or *cochinillo* (suckling pig), so tender that only a fork is needed.

Segovia and the Mountains

This route heads northwest past El Escorial and Segovia, before heading for La Granja and a spectacular mountain pass.

Leave Madrid on the A-6; take the exit for El Escorial. This road becomes the M-505.

The massive palace of El Escorial (► 84) dominates the old town, with its attractive squares and narrow streets.

From El Escorial, route M-600 to Guadarrama passes the entrance to the Valle de los Caídos (► 84) and heads into the tunnel beneath the Puerto de Guadarrama, 1,611m above sea level. Take the N-603 for Segovia.

Don't be put off by the modern outskirts of Segovia, the old heart of the city has an undeniable charm (► 86) and is an excellent place to stop for lunch, with a walk before or afterwards.

From Segovia, the CL-601, signposted Madrid and La Granja, leads up into the hills.

The main attraction in La Granja de San Ildefonso is Felipe V's romantic 18th-century palace, a mini-Versailles. Near by is the Riofrío Palace, built by Felipe's widow, and the **Real Fábrica de Cristales**. In the 18th century, this factory made spectacular chandeliers and mirrors for royal palaces. Today, the craft has been revived in the factory, school and museum.

From La Granja, the CL-601 climbs through peaceful woods, past signs proclaiming ever-increasing altitudes. Admire the view at Puerto de la Navacerrada, a ski resort right at the tree line (1880m). Return to Madrid via the M-601, through Navacerrada, and the N-6.

Distance
200km

Time
9 hours with stops, 5 hours without stops

Start/end point
Madrid
✠ 81D3

Lunch
Cava Duque (€–€€)
✉ Calle de Cervantes 12, Segovia
☎ 921 46 24 87

Real Fábrica de Cristales
✉ Paseo del Pocillo 1, La Granha de San Ildefonso, Segovia
☎ 921 47 18 37
🕐 Wed–Sat 10–6, Sun 10–3
✋ Cheap

The Riofrío Palace at La Granja de San Ildefonso

Above: *a souvenir of Toledo*
Right: *the Puerta de los Leones, on the south side of Toledo Cathedral*

www.guiatoledo.com

✚ 80C1

ℹ Puerta de Bisagra s/n

☎ 925 22 08 43

🕐 Mon–Fri 9–6, Sat 9–7, Sun, public hols 9–3

🍴 Plenty (€–€€)

❓ 50-minute tour through old town on tourist trolley. Starts Plaza de Zocodover

🚌 From 11AM; also at night, weekends

TOLEDO ✪✪✪

Don't miss Toledo. Few cities have such a rich tapestry of art, religion and history. Ironically, a 16th-century painter from Crete is most closely associated with this city, set high on a bluff above the Río Tajo (River Tagus). El Greco (The Greek) painted his greatest works here, including a menacing landscape of the city dominated by its cathedral and fortress. Both still punctuate the skyline of this medieval city, with its steep streets and twisting alleyways.

Toledo is often called the 'city of the three cultures', reflecting the harmony and prosperity enjoyed by Christians, Jews and Muslims during the Middle Ages. The Islamic heritage is recalled in the Moorish architecture, with characteristic keyhole arches and forbidding doors hiding beautiful courtyards. In the Judería (the Jewish quarter), two of the original eight synagogues survive. These were renovated in 1992, along with many houses, five centuries after the expulsion of all Jews from Spain. The cathedral, started in 1226, is one of Spain's largest and after the royal court moved to Madrid in 1560, Toledo remained the country's religious capital.

A mini-lesson in Spanish history, with Roman, Visigoth and Moorish connections, this ancient stronghold became the capital of Castile in 1085. It thrived as a centre of learning, commerce and religious tolerance. Toledo swords and armour were famous throughout Europe. Although there are more than enough museums and churches to admire, the best way to appreciate Toledo is to be there at night after the tourists have left.

Toledo

This atmospheric walk takes in all the important sights. Toledo has steep hills and cobblestone streets, so wear comfortable shoes.

Start at the Plaza de Zocodover.

Through the large Moorish archway under the clock steps lead to the **Museo de Santa Cruz**, a fine museum known for its El Greco paintings. Up the hill on Cuesta Carlos V is the Alcázar fortress.

From the plaza, follow Calle de Comercio. Turn left to the front of the Cathedral.

This enormous Gothic structure is a treasure chest of religious art. The sacristy is hung with works by El Greco, van Dyck and Goya.

Cross the square, follow the alley to the right of the town hall; it narrows into a passageway and you step through a doorway into a tiny square. Turn right on to Calle de El Salvador. Go uphill to Calle de Santo Tomé. Turn left on San Juan de Dios for the Iglesia de Santo Tomé.

Underneath its Moorish tower, the 14th-century church houses El Greco's huge painting, *The Burial of the Count of Orgaz*. Across the square, the **Casa-Museo de El Greco** is dedicated to the famous painter.

From here, Calle de San Juan de Dios leads into the Jewish quarter. Continue to the Sinagoga del Tránsito.

With Moorish and Gothic details, this 14th-century synagogue reflects the three cultures of Toledo; the Sephardic Museum explains the traditions of Spanish Jews.

From here, return to the Plaza de Zocodover or wander through more ancient alleyways.

Toledo's crowning glory, the Alcázar fortress

Distance
1km, hilly

Time
1 hour without stops, 5 hours with stops

Start
Plaza de Zocodover

End
Sinagoga del Tránsito

Lunch
Casa Aurelio (€–€€)
✉ Sinagoga 6
☎ 925 22 20 97

Museo de Santa Cruz
✉ Calle de Cervantes 3
☎ 925 22 10 36
🕐 10–6:30, Sun 10–2
💶 Cheap

Casa-Museo de El Greco
✉ Calle de Samuel Levi 3
☎ 925 22 40 46
🕐 Tue–Sat 10–2, 4–6, Sun 10–2
💶 Cheap

Guadarrama Mountains

Lovely in spring and autumn, this scenic drive north through the green Guadarrama Mountains is also a cool escape from Madrid in the height of summer.

Leave Madrid on the A-6; turn on to the M-608 at Collado Villalba. Continue to Manzanares el Real.

The 15th-century castle at Manzanares el Real (► 85) stands proudly, its battlements, watch-towers and fortifications looking as if they have sprouted from the rock.

The towers and glory of Manzanares el Real, now beautifully restored

Continue on the M-608, turn left on the M-611 for Miraflores de la Sierra.

The road climbs through ranches where massive fighting bulls are bred for the *corrida* (fight). The quiet is broken only by birdsong. In spring and early summer there are wild flowers. On the side of a steep hill, Miraflores is a perfect stop for lunch, with fine views.

Continue on the M-611.

Distance
175km

Time
4 hours, mountain roads

Start/end
Madrid
➕ 81D3

Lunch
Hotel Santa María del Paular
(€€)
✉ N-604, Rascafría
☎ 91 869 10 11

At the pass of Puerto de la Morchera (1,786m), enjoy even more spectacular views across to snowy peaks – even in June. In summer, you pass bushes of wild roses; in autumn, the oaks turn golden brown. The narrow road twists and turns past *refugios*, stone huts for walkers. Just outside Rascafría is a 14th-century monastery; part of it is now a hotel.

At the village of Rascafría, turn right on to the M-604 and continue to Lozoya.

The small village of Lozoya is another good place to stop and stretch your legs before having lunch or a snack.

Follow signs for the N-1 (the E-05), the motorway south to Madrid.

Where To...

Above: *a picture is worth
a thousand words*
Right: *kids just wanna
have fun in the park*

Madrid

Prices

Madrileños say that there is a bank, a pharmacy, a church and a bar on every block. Certainly food and drink are never more than a minute away. Restaurant prices are based on a three-course meal for one, without drinks or service.

€   = under €15
€€   = €15–30
€€€ = over €30

Set Meals

Most restaurants offer a lunchtime *menú del día* (fixed price meal) of around €8 which usually includes an appetizer, main course, dessert and wine or water. This offers great value but limited choice. The price includes VAT but not service; leave 5–10 percent depending on the quality of service. If you eat à la carte, it will cost more, but you can then sample the specialities.

Madrid has well over 17,000 places to eat, but there are times when visitors, especially with children, want somewhere quick, easy and international. The city has several chains of simple but good restaurants that serve meals and snacks with a Spanish accent at low prices. These are open throughout the day, from early in the morning until late into the night.

Angel (€)

Once nicknamed El Comunista for its anti-Franco clientele, this is a well-priced, fun, neighbourhood eatery across from the Mercado de San Antón. At the back are tiny tables with red tablecloths.

✉ **Augusto Figueroa 35** ☎ **91 521 70 12** 🕐 Lunch, dinner. Closed Sun, public hols 🚇 Chueca

El Asador de Aranda (€€)

This restaurant serves the regional speciality of Castile: lamb roasted slowly in a wood-fired oven. Order the local red wines from the province of Madrid.

✉ **Calle Preciados 44** ☎ **91 547 21 56** 🕐 Lunch, dinner. Closed Mon dinner 🚇 Sol

La Barraca (€€)

This is the place for authentic *paella* and other rice-based specialities from the Valencian region. Best accompanied by the white wines from Valencia.

✉ **Calle de la Reina 29** ☎ **91 532 71 54** 🕐 Lunch, dinner 🚇 Banco de España

La Bola (€€)

Behind the Plaza del Oriente, this is the sort of place

where locals bring their out-of-town friends for authentic *cocido madrileño* (Madrid stew). Open since 1870; no credit cards.

✉ **Calle de la Bola 5** ☎ **91 547 69 30** 🕐 Lunch, dinner. Closed Sun dinner 🚇 Santo Domingo

El Botín (➤ 33)

Brasserie de Lista (€–€€)

In the expensive Serrano shopping area, this stylish yet informal restaurant serves international dishes, with grilled meat a speciality.

✉ **Calle Serrano 110** ☎ **91 411 08 64** 🕐 Lunch, dinner. Closed Sat lunch, Sun 🚇 Núñez de Balboa

La Broche (€€€)

Located next to the Hotel Miguel Angel is La Broche, the domain of master chef Sergi Arola, who has won every plaudit going in the last few years, including two Michelin stars. The cuisine is Mediterranean, with a Catalan twist.

✉ **Miguel Angel 29–31** ☎ **91 399 34 37** 🕐 Lunch, dinner. Closed Sat–Sun 🚇 Gregorio Marañon

El Buey (€€€)

Its name means ox, and beef is the speciality, with prime cuts, sold Spanish-style by weight. There are alternative fish dishes. Booking is essential.

✉ **Plaza de la Marina Española 1** ☎ **91 541 30 41** 🕐 Lunch, dinner. Closed Sun dinner 🚇 Opera, Santo Domingo

La Cabaña (€€–€€€)

Charcoal-grilled steaks are the speciality of this pricey,

but reliable Argentinian restaurant, not far from Sol. Tables are in great demand, especially at weekends, so booking is essential.

✉ **Ventura de la Vega 10** ☎ 92 420 17 41 🕐 Lunch, dinner Ⓜ **Sevilla**

Café de la Opera (€€)

Right by the Teatro Real opera house. The waiters and waitresses are opera students, who serve and sing opera and *zarzuela* (light opera). International dishes.

✉ **Calle de Arrieta 6** ☎ 91 542 63 82 🕐 Dinner only Ⓜ **Opera**

Casa Gallega (€€)

Galician restaurants specialize in seafood. Try *sopa de mariscos* (fish soup) or *cogote de merluza* (hake baked in the oven). Also at Plaza de San Miguel, near the market.

✉ **Calle de Bordadores 11** ☎ 91 541 90 55 🕐 Lunch, dinner Ⓜ **Sol**

Casa Lucio (€€)

Popular with the royal family, foreign politicians and film stars. A fashionable but affordable restaurant on Madrid's restaurant row that is known for Castilian dishes such as stews and roasts. Booking essential.

✉ **Calle de la Cava Baja 35** ☎ 91 365 32 52 🕐 Lunch, dinner. Sat dinner only. Closed Aug Ⓜ **La Latina**

A'Casiña (€€)

On a warm day this is an ideal spot for lunch outdoors on the terrace, hidden by greenery from the road through the Casa del Campo. Order Galician specialities, especially seafood. Reservations essential.

✉ **Avenida del Angel, Casa de Campo** ☎ 91 526 34 25 🕐 Lunch, dinner. Closed Sun dinner Ⓜ **Lago**

El Cenador del Prado (€€–€€€)

When you want to try contemporary Spanish cuisine, this is one of the best. Near the Plaza Santa Ana. To enjoy the best of the Heranz brothers, try the *menú de degustación* (special tasting menu).

✉ **Calle del Prado 4** ☎ 91 429 15 61 🕐 Lunch, dinner. Closed Sat lunch, Sun Ⓜ **Antón Martín, Sevilla**

La Chata (€€)

Reputed to be a favourite among bullfighters, the menu features roast suckling pig, lamb and langoustines with sherry sauce or wild mushrooms. Good *tapas* and wines by the glass.

✉ **Cava de la Baja 24** ☎ 91 366 14 58 🕐 Lunch, dinner. Closed Tue, Wed lunch Ⓜ **La Latina**

Cervantes (€–€€)

The wood panelled room behind the bar of Cervantes used to be popular with students on accoount of the affordable menu based on pizza, pasta and crêpes. Prices have gone up a little since the German owner extended the premises, but the homemade cooking is as good as ever.

✉ **Calle Leon 8** ☎ 91 420 12 98 🕐 9AM–1:30AM Ⓜ **Antón Martín**

Las Cuevas de Luis Candelas (€€–€€€)

Just off the Plaza Mayor, this traditional tavern offers Castilian dishes, especially

Opening Times

The Spanish like to eat late. Restaurants tend to serve lunch from 1–3 and dinner from 9–12AM. Cafés are open most of the day and often into the early hours of the morning. *Tapas* bars open from 11–3 and 5 or 6 until late. If you want to sit down to a proper meal in the evening, it is worth phoning ahead to check the opening time and to book a table. During the summer months, particularly August, some establishments close.

Sweets for my Sweet

The *madrileños* love their traditional sweet cakes. During the festival of San Isidro, look out for *rosquillas*, like a ring-shaped doughnut, which comes in several flavours. *Tontas* (stupid) are plain but *listas* (clever) are dipped in sugar and lemon; *Santa Clara* and *Tía Javiera* are soaked in brandy. *Bartolillos* are three-cornered pies. Traditionally eaten during Holy Week, *torrijas* are crunchy, like French toast, but can be enjoyed year-round with a glass of sweet wine at El Rey de los Vinos. At Halloween, pastry shops sell *huesos de santos* (saints' bones) and *buñuelos* (like a doughnut).

roast lamb and pork. Touristy but fun, with plenty of locals, especially for Sunday lunch.

✉ Calle de los Cuchilleros 1 ☎ 91 366 54 28 ⓒ Lunch, dinner ⓜ Sol

Dantxari (€€–€€€)

This Basque tavern has spicy cod, lamb with garlic and wild mushrooms. Wide-ranging Spanish wine list, cheerful service.

✉ Ventura Rodríguez 8 ☎ 91 542 35 24 ⓒ Lunch, dinner. Closed Sun dinner ⓜ Plaza España

Divina La Cocina (€€)

Marinated tuna is the speciality of this stylish, highly innovative establishment in the heart of the Chueca district. Diners choose from a variety of Spanish fusion dishes on the set menu, which is excellent value. Must book ahead.

✉ Colmenares 13 ☎ 91 531 37 65 ⓒ Lunch, dinner ⓜ Chueca

El Estragón (€–€€)

Vegetarion restaurants are still thin on the ground in Madrid. El Estragón has a great location in trendy La Latina, a relaxed ambience and offers reliable veggie standards like stir-fried vegetables and mushroom lasagne.

✉ Plaza de la Paja 10 ☎ 91 365 89 82 ⓒ 12:30PM–12:30AM ⓜ La Latina

Horcher (€€€)

Step back in time to old-fashioned luxury. Wild duck, venison and boar are the specialities in this German-influenced traditional businessmen's haunt.

✉ Alfonso XIII 6 ☎ 91 522 07 31 ⓒ Lunch, dinner. Closed Sat lunch, Sun ⓜ Retiro

Lhardy (€€€)

In 1839, the author of *Carmen* persuaded Emile Lhardy to open a French restaurant in Madrid and it is still going strong. Beautiful, historic and expensive: pheasant with grapes, sole in champagne sauce.

✉ Carrera de San Jerónimo 8 ☎ 91 521 33 85 ⓒ Lunch, dinner. Closed Sun, public hols dinner ⓜ Sevilla, Sol

Malacatín (€–€€)

Despite its echoes of the Franco era, this is still a friendly little spot near the Rastro Flea Market. Another favourite with locals who order *cocido* (Madrid stew).

✉ Calle de la Ruda 5 ☎ 91 365 52 41 ⓒ Lunch, dinner. Closed Sat dinner, Sun, public hols, Jul, Aug ⓜ La Latina

La Panera (€€)

A small corner of Asturias, featuring hearty dishes from northern Spain: *fabada* (pork and beans), *fabes con almejas* (beans and mussels). Order cider.

✉ Calle del Arenal 19 ☎ 91 542 92 20 ⓒ 1–4, 8–12 ⓜ Opera, Sol

La Posada de la Villa (€€–€€€)

An inn since 1642, but now a restaurant famous for its whole roasted milk-fed lamb, baked in a special stone oven just inside the entrance. Close to the Plaza Mayor.

✉ Calle de la Cava Baja 9 ☎ 91 366 18 60 ⓒ Lunch, dinner. Closed Sun dinner, Aug ⓜ La Latina

Mi Pueblo (€€)

Excellent value traditional home cooking (*cocina casera*) is the hallmark of this highly popular, but unpretentious restaurant, only 5 minutes walk from plaza Mayor. The menu comprises a small selection of nourishing meat and fish dishes and you can drink wine from Arganda del Rey (south of Madrid).

✉ **Costanilla de Santiago 2** ☎ **91 548 20 73** 🕙 **Closed Sun eve, Mon** 🚇 **Opera**

Taberna de Antonio Sánchez (€)

Named in honour of the bullfighter Antonio Sánchez, and founded by his father. *Aficionados* meet below the bull's head mounted on the wall of the oldest tavern (1830) in Madrid.

✉ **Calle Mesón de Paredes 13** ☎ **91 539 78 26** 🕙 **Lunch, dinner. Closed Sun dinner** 🚇 **Tirso de Molina**

La Trainera (€€–€€€)

A plain restaurant in the expensive Serrano district, this is one of the best places for fish in Madrid. Try oysters, crabs, *gambas* (prawns), *sopa de mariscos* (fish soup).

✉ **Calle Lagasca 60** ☎ **91 576 80 35** 🕙 **Lunch, dinner. Closed Sun, Aug** 🚇 **Serrano**

La Trucha (€–€€)

Specialising in Andalucian dishes in general and trout in particular, this is the sister restaurant of the *tapas* bar of the same name. Both are just off the Plaza de Santa Ana.

✉ **Calle de Núñez de Arce 6** ☎ **91 532 08 82** 🕙 **Lunch, dinner. Closed Sun, Mon** 🚇 **Sol**

La Vaca Argentina (€–€€€)

Homesick Argentinians come here for big steaks, cooked to perfection. Like its sister restaurants, this branch near the Teatro Real opera house is ranch-style.

✉ **Calle de los Caños del Peral 2** ☎ **91 541 33 18** 🕙 **Lunch, dinner** 🚇 **Opera**

VIPS (€)

A combination shop and restaurant. Menus include familiar dishes, surroundings are cafeteria-style, and you can buy newspapers, film, toiletries and maps.

Viridiana (€€€)

Near the three famous art museums, this is imaginative modern Spanish cooking at its best, thanks to chef Abraham García. Perhaps the best wine list in Spain.

✉ **Calle de Juan de Mena 14** ☎ **91 523 44 78** 🕙 **Lunch, dinner. Closed Sun, public hols, Aug** 🚇 **Banco de España, Retiro**

Viuda de Vacas (€€)

Home-style Castilian cooking, from oxtail to tripe, is the speciality of this oak-beamed restaurant with its twisting staircase, tiles and wood oven.

✉ **Calle de la Cava Alta 23** ☎ **91 366 58 47** 🕙 **Lunch, dinner. Closed Sun dinner, Thu, public hols, Aug** 🚇 **La Latina**

Zalacaín (€€€)

This has a reputation as one of Madrid's top restaurants, with an international menu and Basque specialities. Advance booking essential.

✉ **Calle de Alvarez de Baena 4** ☎ **91 561 59 35** 🕙 **Lunch, dinner. Closed Sat lunch, Aug, Easter** 🚇 **Gregorio Marañón**

Madrid Specialities

Traditional restaurants in the city have wood-fired ovens where whole milk-fed lamb and suckling pig are slowly and gently roasted. In autumn and winter, look for game, *rabo de toro* (oxtail stew) and *cocido madrileño* (Madrid stew), cooked in a *puchero* (clay pot) on a wood fire.

Tapas Bars

Drinks

Madrid has a dry climate and in summer is very hot, but wherever you are, you are never far from a cold drink. Here are some useful words when you need to slake your thirst.

agua mineral: mineral water
caña: small glass of beer
clara: beer and lemonade (shandy)
cubata: rum and coke
fino: dry sherry
de grifo: draught (beer, vermouth)
tubo: large beer
vermú: vermouth
vino blanco: white wine
vino tinto: red wine

Alkalde (€)

A *tapas* bar with a difference: the Basque name is a clue to the Basque-style *tapas*, which include *tortilla* with red peppers and seafood. Handy for shopping sprees in the upmarket Salamanca district.

✉ **Calle de Jorge Juan 10** ☎ **91 576 33 59** 🕓 **Lunch, dinner. Closed Jul, Aug** 🚇 **Serrrano**

El Almendro 13 (€)

This bar specialises in hearty Andalucian cooking, so ask for a *manzanilla* from Sanlúcar with your *tapas*. If you order a *ración* (large portion), a bell is rung when it is ready.

✉ **Calle del Almendro 13** ☎ **91 365 42 52** 🕓 **Lunch, dinner** 🚇 **La Latina**

El Anciano Rey de los Vinos (€)

Founded in 1909, this bar near the Palacio Real is atmospheric, with mirrors and tiles. Try sugary, crunchy *torrijas*, the surprising speciality that is a perfect partner for their own sweet muscatel wines.

✉ **Calle de Bailén 19** ☎ **97 559 53 32** 🕓 **Lunch, dinner. Closed Sun, Aug** 🚇 **La Latina**

Antigua Casa Angel Sierra (€)

Traditional and decorated in old-Madrid style. This 1917 vermouth bar has painted glass and rows of bottles. Vermouth with (*con sifón*) or without soda, is served from a massive brass tap, as is beer. Simple *tapas* are made in front of you.

✉ **Calle de la Gravina 11** ☎ **91 531 01 26** 🕓 **Lunch, dinner** 🚇 **Chueca**

La Ardosa (€)

Copies of Goya prints line the walls of this atmospheric *taberna*, a reminder that the artist's favourite local once occupied this site. Czech beers are another big draw, as is the interesting selection of *tapas* and *raciones*.

✉ **Calle Colón 13** ☎ **91 521 49 79** 🕓 **11:30AM–1:30PM** 🚇 **Tribunal**

Cañas y Tapas (€)

Popular *taberna* chain with tiled décor and a large, seasonally rotating menu of spanish regional *tapas* (English language available). Branch in Plaza España.

www.tapaspain.com ☎ **902 18 09 18**

Los Caracoles (€)

Handy for the Rastro Flea Market, and therefore especially busy on Sundays, the house speciality is snails, but there are plenty of other *tapas* available, all washed down with cheap red wine or beer.

✉ **Plaza de Cascorro 18** ☎ **91 365 94 39** 🕓 **Lunch, dinner. Closed Sun dinner** 🚇 **La Latina**

Casa del Abuleo (€)

Handy for plaza Santa Ana, 'Grandad's place' is the *tapas* bar for connoisseurs. It dates from 1906 and has retained its no-nonsense, spit and sawdust atmosphere. Wine is usually preferred with shrimp, the house speciality, served grilled (*a la plancha*) or fried in garlic (*al ajillo*).

✉ **Calle Victoria 12** ☎ **91 521 2319** 🕓 **11AM–midnight** 🚇 **Sol**

Casa Alberto (€)

Legend has it that Cervantes

came here while writing *Don Quixote*. Order a *Vermut de Grifo* (draught vermouth drawn from a splendid antique pump) and try the *albóndigas* (meatballs).

⊠ Calle de Las Huertas 18
☎ 91 429 93 56 🕓 Lunch, dinner. Closed Sun dinner, Mon
🚇 Sol, Tirso de Molina

Casa Labra (€)

The birthplace of the PSOE (Spanish Socialist Party) in 1879, this *taberna* reeks of tradition. The speciality is *soldaditos de Pavía*, mouthfuls of deep-fried cod. Off Puerta del Sol.

⊠ Calle de Tetuán 12
☎ 91 531 00 81 🕓 Lunch, dinner. Closed Sun, public hols
🚇 Sol

La Dolores (€)

Traditional *taberna* has preserved its original tiled façade which dates from 1908. Always busy, sometimes to bursting point on account of its famous canapés (ask for *pulgas*).

⊠ Plaza de Jesús 4 ☎ 91 429 22 43 🕓 11AM–1AM 🚇 Antón Martín

Estay (€)

A useful spot for lunch or afternoon tea if you've been shopping in the Salamanca district. Estay specialises in delicious Basque *tapas*, using fresh market produce. The deserts are equally imaginative.

⊠ Calle Hermosilla 46 ☎ 91 578 04 70 🕓 Lunch, dinner. Closed Sun 🚇 Velázquez

Los Gatos (€)

Bags of atmosphere in this locals' haunt, famous for its crazy décor – don't miss the altar server with his collection box. Arrive before 2PM if you want a seat for lunch (mainly *tapas*).

⊠ Calle Jesús 2 ☎ 91 429 30 67 🕓 Lunch, dinner. Closed Sun 🚇 Antón Martín

Las Letras (€)

From the same stable as the restaurant Cenador del Prado, this recently renovated bar specialises in up-market *tapas* – *menu del dia* also available. Additional seating upstairs.

⊠ Calle Echegaray 26 ☎ 91 429 48 43 🕓 Midday–1AM 🚇 Sol

Lhardy (€€)

Best known as a luxury restaurant (► 94). The bar looks like a grocery store but sells everything from hot soup to a delicate *fino* sherry from a silver urn. Near Puerta del Sol.

⊠ Carrera de San Jerónimo 8
☎ 91 521 33 85 🕓 Lunch, dinner. Closed Sun, public hols dinner 🚇 Sol, Sevilla

Museo Chicote (► 54)

Taberna de Cien Vinos (€)

This 'tavern of 100 wines' in one of the oldest parts of town has a lively clientele. Join them to sample a wide range of Spanish wines.

⊠ Calle del Nuncio 17 ☎ 91 365 47 04 🕓 Lunch, dinner. Closed Mon 🚇 La Latina

La Trucha (€)

Just off the Plaza Santa Ana, this is a sister of the nearby restaurant. Regulars stand at the bar, drinking chilled red house wine by the glass and sampling a wide array of *tapas*. Choose fish, meat or vegetables grilled *a la plancha*.

⊠ Calle Manuel Fernández y González 3 ☎ 91 429 58 33
🕓 Lunch, dinner
🚇 Antón Martín, Sevilla

Viva Madrid (€)

You can't miss this bar, with its tiled picture of Cybeles outside. The clientele is young and lively. Just off Plaza de Santa Ana.

⊠ Calle Manuel Fernández y González 7 ☎ 91 429 36 40
🕓 Lunch, dinner 🚇 Sevilla

Tapas

There are hundreds of combinations of *tapas*. Here are a few of the most common.
albóndigas: meatballs
callos: tripe
croquetas: potato croquettes
gambas: prawns
jamón: dried ham
mojama: dried tuna
morcilla: black pudding
pescaíto, *boquerones*, *chanquetes*: fried fish
pimientos rellenos: stuffed red peppers
tortilla: potato omelette

Cafés and Bars with a Difference

Coffee

Drinking coffee is a way of life in Madrid. A small, black espresso is a *café solo*, a weaker, American-style coffee is an *americano*, while black with just a splash of milk is a *cortado* ('cut' with milk). Milky coffee, which is usually only taken with breakfast, is *café con leche*. Decaffeinated coffee is more readily available than it used to be: ask for *descafeinado*. In summer a *café con hielo* (iced black coffee) is surprisingly refreshing.

Alhambra (€)

A lively taberna with a relaxed Andalucian ambience, handy for the nightspots of Sol and Santa Ana. Friendly staff serve a good selection of *tostadas* and other *tapas*.

✉ Calle Victoria 9 ☎ 91 521 07 08 🕐 11AM–2AM. Closed Mon lunch 🚇 Sol

El Balcón de Rosales (€)

On the pretty *paseo* overlooking the Casa de Campo, this disco-bar is popular with the younger set who come here for Tex-Mex food. Even the Spanish love karaoke.

✉ Paseo del Pintor Rosales ☎ 91 541 74 40 🕐 8PM–dawn. Closed Mon–Wed 🚇 Argüelles

Café de los Austrias (€)

Portraits of royals and marble tables help to recreate the Madrid of 100 years ago. This busy and popular café is big and bright and overlooks the square.

✉ Plaza de Ramales 1 ☎ 91 559 84 36 🕐 9AM–1AM. Closed Mon PM 🚇 Opera

Café del Foro (€)

Tiny *copas* bar with arresting tiled décor. Serves canapés but if you're really hungry there's a restaurant at the back with occasional live music.

✉ Calle San Andrés 38 ☎ 91 445 37 52 🕐 7PM–3AM 🚇 Bilbao

Café Gijon (€)

Open since 1888 and still one of Madrid's most popular meeting places, particularly for those in the film and theatre industry. A well-priced *menu del día* as well as snacks.

✉ Paseo de Recoletos 21 ☎ 91 521 54 25 🕐 8AM–1:30AM 🚇 Banco de España, Colón

Café Isadora (€)

This fashionable bar is the ideal place to enjoy a quiet drink with friends. The décor pays tribute to the famous American dancer, Isadora Duncan. Snacks available as well as cocktails and unusual liqueur coffees.

✉ Calle Divino Pastor 14 ☎ 91 445 71 54 🕐 4PM–2AM 🚇 Bilbao

Café Manuela (€)

Popular, grandiose-looking student haunt which doubles as a kind of club for visitors who want to brush up their Spanish or locals who read the papers and play board games. Serves cocktails snacks and draught beer.

✉ Calle San Vicente Ferrer 29 ☎ 91 531 70 37 🕐 6PM–2AM 🚇 Tribunal

Café de Oriente (€)

It doesn't matter what time your tour of the Palacio Real finishes, this elegant café will be open, serving *tapas*, sandwiches, pizzas and *pâtisseries*. Sit outdoors in summer.

✉ Plaza de Oriente 2 ☎ 91 541 39 74 🕐 8:30AM–1:30AM, weekends to 2:30AM 🚇 Opera

Café & Té (€)

With colourful walls and straw hats, the theme is Colombian. There are some eight branches in this growing chain. As well as coffee and tea, they sell milk shakes, *frappés* (cold iced drinks) and snacks.

Cervecería Alemana (€)
Yet another watering-hole where Hemingway once drank, this 1904 German-style beer house even uses steins. Wood panelling and white marble-topped tables add to the atmosphere.
✉ **Plaza de Santa Ana 6**
☎ **91 429 70 33**
🕐 **11AM–12:30AM, Fri, Sat to 2AM. Closed Tue, Aug**
🚇 **Antón Martín, Sevilla, Sol**

Cervecía Santa Barbara (€)
Business men and women flock to this large beer hall after finishing a day's work. Can be a little frenetic at times, but thus doesn't put off Madrileños who rate the draught lager, dark beer and seafood *tapas*.
✉ **Plaza de Santa Barbara 8**
☎ **91 319 04 49**
🕐 **9AM–midnight** 🚇 **Alonso Martinez**

Chocolatería San Ginés (€)
All green tiles and mirrors, this small café is a favourite for hot chocolate and *churros*. At 3:30AM it is packed with partygoers from the nightclub next door.
✉ **Pasadizo de San Ginés 5**
☎ **91 365 65 46** 🕐 **7PM–7AM**
🚇 **Sol**

Embassy (€)
Founded in 1931, this sophisticated boulevard café-tea room has its own *pâtisserie*, specialising in mouth-watering, French-style cakes. It also serves cocktails and elegant snacks. Branches at Ayala 3 and La Moraleja.
✉ **Paseo de la Castellana 12**
☎ **91 435 94 80** 🕐 **9:30AM– 1AM** 🚇 **Colón, Serrano**

El Espejo (€)
Espejo means 'mirror', and the tall, elegant mirrors are just part of the appeal of this art nouveau café on the stylish part of the

paseo. Choose one of the outdoor tables and enjoy people-watching.
✉ **Paseo de Recoletos 31**
☎ **91 308 23 47**
🕐 **10:30AM–1AM** 🚇 **Banco de España, Colón**

Museo del Jamón (€–€€)
This 30-year-old family enterprise has five downtown branches, hung with thousands of dried Serrano hams. Expect light meals, pastries and coffee, as well as fresh bread to take away.

Pans & Company (€)
This chain sells Spanish-style fast food, as well as hot, wholemeal and grilled sandwiches, salads, ice-creams and cold drinks.

Parnasillo (€)
A busy cocktail and snack bar in the heart of the atmospheric Malasaña district. The décor from the belle époque period is the other attraction.
✉ **Calle San Andrés 33** ☎ **91 447 00 79** 🕐 **3:30PM–3AM** 🚇 **Bilbao**

Populart (€)
Late-night live music is the speciality at this 'Café Jazz'. Expect to pay a small cover charge to listen to jazz plus anything from flamenco to reggae.
✉ **Calle de las Huertas 22**
☎ **91 429 84 07**
🕐 **4PM– 2:30AM** 🚇 **Antón Martín**

La Venencia (€)
If a chair is propping the door ajar, this 1929 bar is open for business. Sample sherries, from the sweetest to the driest. Simple *tapas*, *mojama* (salty dried tuna) and olives.
✉ **Calle de Echegaray 7**
☎ **91 429 73 13** 🕐 **Lunch, dinner. Closed Aug**
🚇 **Sevilla, Sol**

Cheers!
In most bars, inexpensive red wine is the norm, served in a *chato*, which is about the size of a shot glass. However, Madrid has a number of bars that specialise in *vermút*, slightly bitter but refreshing draught vermouth drawn from a barrel, either straight or *con sifón* (with soda water). Bars that have an Andalucian flavour specialise in sherry, and you can choose anything from dry *finos* to sweet *olorosos*.

Outside Madrid

Spanish Regional Dishes

Madrid is an international city, with the cuisines of the world represented, but there are also restaurants and cafés serving food from all regions of Spain. The Valencian style of cooking means rice-based dishes, especially *paella*. In Asturias, *sidra* (cider) is used in cooking and is also drunk with the meals. Both Galicia and the Basque country are well known for the excellence of their fish and shellfish. Catalan cooking tends to be innovative and Mediterranean. Always ask for the regional wine that goes with these regional dishes.

Alcalá de la Henares
Hostería del Estudiante (€€)
In one of the 15th-century student colleges, now restored and a restaurant serving Castilian dishes.
✉ Calle de los Colegios 3
☎ 91 888 03 30 🕐 Lunch, dinner. Closed Aug

Aranjuez
Casa José (€)
To eat asparagus and strawberries where they are grown there's nowhere better than this high-class restaurant, regarded as the best in town.
✉ Calle de los Abastos 32
☎ 91 891 14 88 🕐 Lunch, dinner. Closed Sun dinner, Mon

Chinchón
Parador Nacional de Turismo (€–€€)
Just off the Plaza Mayor, this converted former convent and cloisters is a delightful oasis of calm and elegance. Fine restaurant, local dishes.
✉ Calle Generalísimo 1
☎ 91 894 08 36 🕐 Lunch, dinner

El Escorial
Parilla del Príncipe (€–€€)
A restaurant set in an 18th-century palace. Fish dishes make a welcome change from the typical mountain fare of so many restaurants.
✉ Calle de Floridablanca 6
☎ 91 890 16 11 🕐 Lunch, dinner

Charoles (€€€)
Classy restaurant famed for its traditional cooking including the nourishing stew *cocido madrileño*, recommended by the Spanish gastronomy association (Mon–Fri only).
✉ Calle Floridablanca 24

☎ 91 890 59 75 🕐 Lunch, dinner.

La Granja de San Ildefonso
Restaurante Zaca (€)
Eating here is like eating in a Spanish home, with hearty dishes such as ox tongue and stews. Family-run for 60 years. Worth booking.
✉ Calle de los Embajadores 6
☎ 92 147 00 87 🕐 Lunch only

El Pardo
La Marquesita (€€)
Game and roast meats are the specialities of this old restaurant near the Pardo Palace.
✉ Avenida de la Guardia 29
☎ 91 376 03 77 🕐 Lunch, dinner

Segovia
La Floresta (€€)
Eat roast suckling pig in one of the small dining rooms or in the courtyard among a fountain and flowers.
✉ Calle de San Agustín 27
☎ 921 46 33 14 🕐 Lunch, dinner

Toledo
La Abadía (€–€€)
Next to the Iglesia de San Nicolás, this informal restaurant is in the brick cellar of a 16th-century mansion. Above-average cooking, and unusual *tapas*.
✉ Plaza San Nicolás 3 ☎ 925 25 07 46 🕐 Lunch, dinner

Casón de los López de Toledo (€€)
Lamb with figs is among the enterprising dishes served here. Courtyard with plants downstairs; upstairs is the elegant dining-room.
✉ Calle de la Sillería 3 ☎ 925 25 47 74 🕐 Lunch, dinner

Madrid

El Antiguo Convento (€€€)
This refurbished 17th-century convent has tastefully decorated rooms overlooking the cloisters and a tranquil garden. Expensive, but well worth the outlay for a special stay.
www.elconvento.net
✉ Calle de las Monjas, Boadilla del Monte ☎ 91 632 22 20 🚌 514

Apartohotel Eraso (€)
This 3-star hotel in the Salamanca district,is good value for families and has 31 modern rooms. Own garage.
www.aphotel-eraso.com
✉ Calle de Ardemans 13 ☎ 91 355 32 00, fax 91 355 66 52 🚇 Diego de León

Casa de Madrid (€€€)
A small exclusive hotel, only a short walk from the Royal Palace, owned by art historian and interior designer, Marta Medina Muro. The décor of the 18th-century building includes portraits, antique furniture and Piranesi prints.
www.casademadrid.com
✉ Calle Arreita 2 ☎ 91 559 57 91 🚇 Opera

Hotel Alcalá (€€–€€€)
This 146-room hotel has surprisingly stylish rooms with lots of polished wood. Helpful staff.
www.nh-hoteles.es ✉ Calle de Alcalá 66 ☎ 91 435 10 60 🚇 Príncipe de Vergara

Hotel Asturias (€)
Over 100 years old, this 170-room hotel is good for bargain accommodation in the middle of the city.
www.chh.es
✉ Calle de Sevilla 2 ☎ 91 429 66 76 🚇 Sevilla

Hotel Emperador (€€)
With 241 rooms right in the middle of town, this is popular with package tour organisers, but the rooms are spacious and there is the bonus of a roof-top pool.
www.emperadorhotel.com
✉ Gran Vía 53 ☎ 91 547 28 00, fax 91 547 28 17 🚇 Gran Vía

Hostal Kryse (€)
Handy for sightseeing and shopping, these two-hostals-in-one offer good value. Rooms are clean, reasonably sized and have ensuite bathroom, TV and ceiling fan.
✉ Calle Fuencarral 25 1°
☎ 91 531 1512 🚇 Gran via

Hotel Lagasca (€€)
A 3-star hotel near the shops of the Serrano and surrounded by good restaurants. Opened in the early 1990s, its 100 rooms are plain, in minimalist style; striking bathrooms.
www.nh-hoteles.com
✉ Calle de Lagasca 64 ☎ 91 575 46 06, fax 91 575 16 94 🚇 Velázquez

Hotel Moderno (€€)
This 3-star hotel is only moments from the Plaza Mayor and the Puerta del Sol. Families welcome.
www.hotelmoderno.com
✉ Calle del Arenal 2 ☎ 91 531 09 00 🚇 Sol

Hotel Moncloa Garden (€€)
A modern 3-star hotel, popular with business people during the week and overseas holidaymakers at weekends. Handy for the Metro, breakfast buffet.
www.hotelmoncloagarden.com
✉ Calle Serrano Jover 1 ☎ 91 542 45 82 🚇 Argüelles, Ventura Rodríguez

Prices
Prices are based on the cost of a double room per night. Rates rarely include breakfast or tax.
€ = under €100
€€ = €100–150
€€€ = over €150
Although most hotels have air-conditioning, it is worth double-checking that your room will be cool during the summer months. If the hotel is on a main street, ask for a room at the back.

Money-saving Tip
If you are going to Madrid for a weekend, you can often get a reduced rate. Another money-saving system is run by Bancotel, who have 300 participating hotels in Spain. Buy a Bancotel chequebook with five cheques and you can save up to 65 percent on the usual rates. For details, ☎ 906 321 322 (Spain), +34 915 096 109 (international), www.bancotel.com, or call your local travel agent. They also offer reductions on car hire and golf.

Hotel Opera (€–€€)
A smart, contemporary 3-star hotel handy for the Teatro Real, the Palacio Real (► 23) and the old quarter. Public parking near by.
www.hotelopera.com
✉ Cuesta de Santo Domingo 2
☎ 91 541 28 00, fax 91 541 69 23 🚇 Opera

Hotel Orense (€€)
Just off the Paseo de la Castellana and near the Real Madrid football stadium, this 140-room, 4-star hotel is also ideal for the business district.
www.hotelorense.com
✉ Calle de Pedro Teixeira 5
☎ 91 597 15 68, fax 91 597 12 95 🚇 Estadio Bernabéu

Hotel Palace (€€€)
Built in 1913, this Westin 5-star hotel lives up to its name, from the stained-glass dome over the huge lobby to the gymnasium, garage, two restaurants and 144 rooms. A short walk from Madrid's three famous art museums.
www.palacemadrid.com
✉ Plaza de las Cortes 7
☎ 91 360 80 00, fax 91 360 81 00 🚇 Banco de España

Hotel Ritz, Madrid (€€€)
Dating from 1910, this was the first grand, international hotel in Madrid. Five stars, 156 rooms, three restaurants, one in the flower-filled garden, and a fitness centre. Enjoy a luxurious, if expensive experience, near museums and Retiro Park (► 24).
www.lemeridien-ritzmadrid.com
✉ Plaza de la Lealtad 5
☎ 91 701 67 67, fax 91 701 67 76 🚇 Banco de España

Hotel Santo Mauro (€€€)
Models and pop stars check in to this former palace for peace and style. All 36 rooms are individually decorated, with modern furnishings.

Marble fireplaces and an old library hark back to the 19th century.
www.ac-hoteles.com
✉ Calle de Zurbano 36
☎ 91 319 69 00, fax 91 308 54 77 🚇 Rubén Darío

Hotel Suecia (€€)
Practical rather than pretty, the Suecia has 128 modern rooms and a seventh floor terrace for sunbathing.
www.hotelsuecia.com
✉ Calle del Marqués de Casa Riera 4 ☎ 91 531 69 00, fax 91 521 71 41
🚇 Banco de España

Hotel Tryp Monte Real (€€–€€€)
On the northwest edge of Madrid, near the Puerta de Hierro golf course and the motorway. With 80 luxury rooms, this quiet 5-star hotel is ideal for business meetings. The Real Madrid footballers stay here before big matches.
www.solmelia.com
✉ Calle del Aroyo Fresno 17
☎ 91 316 21 40, fax 91 316 39 34

Hotel Tryp Reina Victoria (€€€)
You can't miss the ornate tower of this 4-star hotel, with 201 rooms, where bullfighters traditionally stay. Overlooks the bars and cafés of the Plaza de Santa Ana.
www.trypreinavictoria.solmelia.com ✉ Plaza de Santa Ana 14 ☎ 91 531 45 00, fax 91 522 03 07 🚇 Sol

Hotel Villa Magna (€€€€)
Stars of the film and pop world stay here in 5-star luxury, near the main business district and upmarket Calle de Serrano shopping. There are 182 rooms, two restaurants, plus 350-space car park.
www.madrid.hyatt.com
✉ Paseo de la Castellana 22
☎ 91 587 12 34, fax 91 575 31 58 🚇 Colón

Outside Madrid

Alcala de Henares

Hospederia La Tercia (€€)
Small but charming hotel (14 rooms) situated in a 17th-century listed building near the University. Comfortable, well equipped rooms, restaurant and terrace.
www.latercia.com

✉ Calle La Tercia 8 ☎ 91 879 68 00; fax 91 879 66 62

Chinchón

Parador Nacional de Turismo (€€–€€€)
Get away from it all in this converted 15th-century convent. Wander in the gardens, with their pear trees and jasmine, or swim the pool. Elegant restaurant (► 83).
www.parador.es

✉ Calle Generalísimo 1
☎ 91 894 08 36, fax 91 894 09 08

El Escorial

Hotel Victoria Palace (€€–€€€)
A grand 4-star hotel with 90 rooms, just 200m from the famous monastery-palace. Swimming pool, restaurants.
www.hotelvictoriapalace.com

✉ Calle de Juan de Toledo 4
☎ 91 890 15 11, fax 91 890 12 48

Parilla del Príncipe (€)
A restaurant with rooms (► 100) in an 18th-century palace. The 23 bedrooms are simple but comfortable.
www.inicia.es

✉ Calle de Floridablanca 6
☎ 91 890 16 11

Segovia

Ayala Berganza (€€)
A 15th-century palace converted into a stylish, modern 4-star hotel. The look is minimalist, with the ancient walls and arches adding character. Luxurious bedrooms, private parking.
www.partner-hotels.com

✉ Calle de Carretas 5 ☎ 92 146 04 48, fax 92 146 23 77

Hotel Infanta Isabel (€)
Converted to a hotel in 1992, this 19th-century building overlooks the Plaza Mayor. Ask for a room with a balcony so that you can admire the cathedral. Good breakfast but no restaurant.
www.infantaisabel.com

✉ Plaza Mayor ☎ 92 146 13 00, fax 92 146 22 17

Parador de Segovia (€€)
A 113-room hotel surrounded by trees and lawns, only 3km from Segovia's famous aqueduct. Restaurant, gymnasium, sauna and two swimming pools.
www.parador.es

✉ Carretera de Valladolid
☎ 92 144 37 37, fax 92 143 73 62

Toledo

Hostal del Cardenal (€)
What was once the home of the powerful archbishops of Toledo is now a 27-room hotel. Eighteenth-century touches remain, as does the lovely garden. The restaurant is highly rated.
www.hostaldelcardenal.com

✉ Paseo de Recaredo 24
☎ 92 522 49 00, fax 92 522 29 91

Parador del Conde de Orgaz (€€)
The best feature of this modern hillside hotel is its sunset views of the city across the river. The 148 bedrooms are plain, but comfortable. The restaurant serves local specialities.
www.parador.es

✉ Paseo de los Cigarrales
☎ 92 522 18 50, fax 92 522 51 66

The Paradores of Spain
Spain has long been famous for its *paradores*, a government-run chain of hotels. These are often converted castles and monasteries in attractive locations with reasonably priced rooms. They make a point of serving regional dishes in their restaurants. Central reservations
☎ 91 516 66 66, fax 91 516 66 57;
www.parador.es

Clothes, Jewellery & Accessories

Department Stores

Spain's most popular department store group is El Corte Inglés. As well as fashion, fabrics and accessories, they sell everything from toiletries to camera film and batteries. With well-priced restaurants, they are usually open from 10–9, and do not close for lunch. Central branches include:
Calle de Preciados 3
Plaza de Callao 2
Calle de Goya 76 and 87
Calle de Raimundo
  Fernandez Villaverde 79
Calle de la Princesa 42
Calle de Serrano 47

Fashion for Men and Women

Adolfo Domínguez

Although the top international designers are represented in Madrid, Spain has its own superstars. Adolfo Domínguez has seven fashion and accessory shops, including several in the Serrano shopping area.
✉ Calle de Serrano 18
☎ 91 577 82 80
Ⓜ Serrano

Agatha Ruiz de la Prada

When you are looking for something out of the ordinary, whether for men or women, this store could be just the place. Just off the Paseo de la Castellana.
✉ Calle del Marqués del Riscal 8 ☎ 91 310 44 83
Ⓜ Rubén Darío

Cortefiel Hombre and Cortefiel Mujer

One of the most popular chains, selling men's and women's clothing. There are eight branches in Madrid selling everything from designer fashions to reasonably priced, everyday wear.
✉ Calle de Serrano 40, Grand Via 27 ☎ 91 431 33 42 Ⓜ Serrano

Homeless

As the name implies, this elegant boutique started out in 1994 raising money for the homeless of San Sebastian. It now has its own label offering casual clothing mainly to young professionals. There's another branch on Calle Serrano.
www.homeless.es
✉ Calle Fuencarral 16
☎ No phone Ⓜ Gran Via

Jésus del Pozo

Near the Plaza de Cibeles and off the Paseo de Recoletos, this shop features one of Spain's leading and most famous young designers.
✉ Calle del Almirante 9
☎ 91 531 36 46
Ⓜ Colón

Lemon

Fun boutique in this increasingly trendy shopping street, selling embroidered trousers, patchwork bags and other accessories.
✉ Calle Fuencarral 37 ☎ 91 532 47 01 Ⓜ Gran Via

Mango

At last count, there were nine branches of this highly successful chain, selling stylish clothes in stylish settings. Mainly for the young and young-at-heart, who recognise good value when they see it.
✉ Calle de Goya 83
☎ 91 435 39 58
Ⓜ Goya

Mitsuoko

This chic store has a great selection of international labels, including Indian Rose, DKNY, Sybilla etc. When you've finished shopping, pop upstairs for a plate of sushi in the café.
✉ Calle Fuencarral 59 ☎ 91 532 73 85 Ⓜ Tribunal

Purification Garcia

The famous Spanish designer's Salamanca store showcases an alluring range of *pret-a-porter* men and women's clothing, as well as accessories.
✉ Calle Serrano 28 & 92
☎ 91 435 80 13/91 576 72 76
Ⓜ Serrano, Nuñez de Balboa

Roberto Verino

This Spanish designer has several stores in central Madrid, with clothes and accessories for men and women.

- ✉ **Calle de Claudio Coello 27**
- ☎ **91 577 73 81**
- Ⓜ **Serrano**

Yanko

Yanko's elegant shoes are well known all across Spain and sold in major department stores. Their flagship store displays their latest men's and women's designs.

- ✉ **Calle de Lagasca 52**
- ☎ **91 576 16 78**
- Ⓜ **Serrano**

Zara

Up-to-the-minute styles at low prices have made this chain of stores a success not just in Spain but internationally as well. This is one of five branches in Madrid.

- ✉ **Gran Vía 32**
- ☎ **91 522 97 27** Ⓜ **Gran Vía**

Fans and Capes

Casa de Diego

Most women in Madrid still carry a fan in their handbag for hot weather or as a fashion accessory. This old-fashioned fan and umbrella shop sells a huge range; the best are works of art, costing as much as a painting.

- ✉ **Puerta del Sol 12**
- ☎ **91 522 66 43** Ⓜ **Sol**

Seseña

The cape is both Spanish and romantic. For about 100 years, Seseña has been famous for its ready-made and tailor-made capes for men and women.

- ✉ **Calle de la Cruz 23**
- ☎ **91 531 68 40**
- Ⓜ **Sol**

Jewellery

Ansorena

In business for over 150 years and jewellers to the royal family in that time, Ansorena is synonymous with fine jewellery in Madrid. Everything from ropes of pearls to diamond-studded tiaras are on display at their glamorous store.

- ✉ **Calle de Alcalá 52 and 54**
- ☎ **91 532 85 15**
- Ⓜ **Banco de España**

Anuxa

Earrings, bracelets and other jewellery with simple, but arresting original designs are among the accessories on sale here.

- ✉ **Calle Hortaleza 8**
- ☎ **91 360 41 73**
- Ⓜ **Gran Vía**

Leather Goods

Camper

Madrid is full of shoe shops, but this is one of the most popular, part of a country-wide chain. Well-priced, good styles for men and women, including some that are fun and just that little bit different.

- ✉ **Calle de Ayala 13**
- ☎ **91 431 43 45**
- Ⓜ **Serrano**

Las Bailarinas

Brightly painted shoes with original designs from Monica García are the speciality of this Chueca store which also sells bags and other fashion accessories.

- ✉ **Calle Piamonte 19**
- ☎ **91 319 90 69**
- Ⓜ **Chueca**

Loewe

Enrique Loewe started a leather goods shop in Calle Echegaray back in 1846. Since then the company has won the title of Proveedora de la Real Casa (By Royal Appointment) and is still a world-famous leader for quality.

- ✉ **Calle de Serrano 26 and 34**
- ☎ **91 577 60 56**
- Ⓜ **Gran Vía**

Shopping Areas

The best-known, and most expensive, shopping area of Madrid is on and around the Calle de Serrano (► 34). Other good hunting grounds include the Gran Vía, and the area around Puerta del Sol, especially Calle de Preciados. Near the University, on the northwest side of the city, Calle de la Princesa has young, trendy shops. Around Chueca, new boutiques and galleries are opening every day.

Arts, Crafts, Gifts & Design

Palacios y Museos
This is the place to buy reproductions of famous pieces from the world's most famous museums. Typically Spanish gifts include decanters based on designs from the 18th-century glass factory at La Granja, gold cufflinks based on pre-Colombian artefacts, and fans made of polished pear wood.
 Arturo Soria 126
☎ 91 338 72 65

El Angel
Spain is known for its shops selling religious items, ranging from pictures of saints and nativity scenes to nuns' habits. El Angel is one of the best.
✉ Calle de Esparteros 3
☎ 91 532 04 91 🔘 Sol

Antigua Casa Crespo
This old-fashioned shop is known for selling *alpargatas*, espadrilles, or rope-soled shoes, that come in all shapes and sizes. You can also buy leather sandals here.
✉ Calle del Divino Pastor 29
☎ 91 521 56 54
🔘 San Bernardo, Bilbao

El Arco de los Cuchilleros
In the heart of the tourist district, this building houses 30 or more craftsmen and women, producing contemporary jewellery, textiles and ceramics. Well priced and well worth a look.
✉ Plaza Mayor 9
☎ 91 365 26 80 🔘 Sol

B D Ediciones de Diseño
Best known for showcasing the finest of Spanish and international furniture designers. Also sells smaller items such as trays, pitchers and chic kitchenware.
 Calle de Villanueva 5
☎ 91 435 54 53
🔘 Serrano, Retiro

Cántaro
Spanish pottery and ceramics always make good souvenirs and presents. This shop near the Gran Vía has a wide range, representing every corner of Spain. The only difficulty is making a choice!
✉ Calle de la Flor Baja 8
☎ 91 547 95 14 🔘 Santo
Domingo, Plaza de España

La Casa de los Chales
Spanish shawls, with their characteristic embroidery and fringe, come in all sorts of fabrics and a multitude of designs. Prices are just as broad ranging. Here, you can choose from wool as well as velvet and lace.
✉ Calle de Maiquez 3
☎ 91 409 72 39 🔘 Goya

Casa Jiménez
Spanish *mantillas* may not be a practical gift for visitors from foreign countries, but *mantonas* (shawls) can make useful and attractive presents. The shawls in this well-known specialist shop are often described as works of art. Find it just off the Gran Vía.
✉ Calle de Preciados 42
☎ 91 548 05 26 🔘 Callao

Expresion Negra
A fascinating emporium dealing in everything associated with African arts and crafts. You can pick up items like patchwork quilts, briefcases, woven baskets, rugs and much more besides.
 Calle Piamonte 15
☎ 91 319 95 27 🔘 Chueca

El Flamenco Vive
The de la Plaza family claim that this is the only shop dedicated to the art of flamenco or what they call the Spanish 'blues'. They sell everything from guitars to memorabilia. Buy some shoes, a video and an instruction book and you're ready to learn to dance.
✉ Calle de Conde de Lemos 7
☎ 91 547 39 17 🔘 Opera

Gion
Near the Real Madrid football stadium, the speciality here

is exquisite embroidered silk kimonos, surrounded by handicrafts from the Kyoto region of Japan, from where the owner hails.

☒ **Calle Orense 30**
☎ **91 556 90 78**
Ⓜ **Santiago Bernabéu**

La Mansión del Fumador
Everything for the smoker, from pipes to ash trays and from lighters to cigar cutters. Surprisingly, they do not sell tobacco.

☒ **Calle del Carmen 22**
☎ **91 532 08 17** Ⓜ **Sol**

María José Fermín
This traditional wrought-iron worker is on the street that becomes the Rastro Flea Market (► panel) on Sunday. In addition to barbecues, chairs and tables, he makes attractive weather vanes adorned with cockerels and witches.

☒ **Ribera de Curtidores 9**
☎ **91 539 43 67** Ⓜ **La Latina**

Museo Nacional Centro de Arte Reina Sofía
The excellent shop has the widest range of modern art books in the city, as well as cheap mementos such as *Guernica* key rings and pencil cases.

☒ **Calle Santa Isabel 52**
☎ **91 467 50 62** Ⓜ **Atocha**

Museo Thyssen-Bornemisza
Down in the gift shop of this museum is a wide choice of reproductions of the most famous paintings in the museum. Best sellers include Gauguin's hot-coloured South Pacific scene, *Mata Mua* (1892); find it on everything from expensive silk scarves to simple posters.

☒ **Paseo del Prado 8**

☎ **91 420 39 44** Ⓜ **Banco de España**

Pérez A Fernández
It's worth going along to this century-old silversmiths, just to look at the exterior of this beautiful shop. Inside, the handcrafted silver is based on traditional Galician designs.

☒ **Calle de Zaragoza 3**
☎ **91 366 42 79** Ⓜ **Opera**

Popland
You could spend hours here, window shopping the crazy miscellany of 1950s and 60s popular kitsch – everything from Judy Garland cut-out dolls to James Bond posters and Beatles figurines.

☒ **Calle Manuela Malasaña 7**
☎ **91 446 38 95**
Ⓜ **Tribunal**

Quetzal
A wide range of crafts imported from India and Nepal, plus others from South and Central America.

☒ **Calle Mayor 13**
☎ **91 364 25 76** Ⓜ **Sol**

Santa
An Aladdin's cave of delights for chocolate lovers, this Salamanca store sells over 60 varieties including pralines, truffles, marron glaces and a giant 50 gram bobon. The speciality however is *leña vieja* (chocolates shaped like logs and sold at Christmas time).

☒ **Calle de Serrano 56**
☎ **91 576 86 46** Ⓜ **Serrano**

El Tintero
In the heart of Chueca, this clothing store specializes in T-shirts with original designs.

☒ **Calle Gravina 5, 9**
☎ **91 308 14 18** Ⓜ **Chueca**

Rastro Flea Market
The Sunday morning El Rastro is legendary (► 65). Many stalls sell modern handicrafts, such as model planes and boats made from recycled soft drink cans, scented candles, wood carvings and leather belts and handbags. This is a good place to shop for inexpensive souvenirs and gifts.

Antiques, Books & Music

Read All About It!
Wander along Calle de Claudio Moyano, on the south side of the Real Jardín Botánico (➤ 70), to have a look at the stalls of the Mercado del Libro. This open-air, second-hand book market is busiest on Sunday mornings, but some stalls are open during the week. At the end of May and beginning of June, *La Feria del Libro* (Madrid's book fair), attracts crowds to Parque del Retiro, where hundreds of stalls representing publishers and bookshops are set up.

La Casa del Libro
The largest bookstore in Spain, with five floors in a classic art nouveau building. As well as thousands of Spanish titles, there is a useful corner selling books and guides in several foreign languages.
- ✉ **Gran Vía 29**
- ☎ **91 521 21 13**
- Ⓜ **Gran Vía**

Casa Postal
The postcards we send today are the collectors' items of tomorrow. This old-fashioned shop is a rummagers delight, crammed with old and antique postcards, as well as maps, photographs and 'curiosities', such as train sets and unused calendars from 1949. Any special requests are ably handled by Martín Carrasco Marqués, the proud owner.
- ✉ **Calle de la Libertad 37**
- ☎ **91 532 70 37**
- Ⓜ **Chueca**

Félix Manzanero
What could be more Spanish than the guitar? Manzanero served an apprenticeship with the legendary José Ramirez and now has his own shop, where both professionals and amateurs come to buy handcrafted instruments. He also has on display antique guitars, dating back to the 18th century.
- ✉ **Calle de Santa Ana 12**
- ☎ **91 366 00 47**
- Ⓜ **La Latina, Tirso de Molina**

Felix Antigüedades
This antiques dealer in the heart of the Rastro flea market specialises in Oriental art, objets d'art after 1700 and musical instruments.
- ✉ **Plaza General Vara del Rey 3** ☎ **91 528 48 30**
- Ⓜ **La Latina**

Galerías Piquer
Most of the score of antique shops that overlook the quiet courtyard have old-fashioned, rather heavy Spanish antiques. Go during the week to avoid the crowds on a Sunday.
- ✉ **Calle de Ribera de Curtidores 29**
- Ⓜ **La Latina, Puerta de Toledo**

International Bookshop
A useful shop for foreign visitors, this is a treasure trove of mostly second-hand books in every category you can think of and in half a dozen different languages.
- ✉ **Calle de Campomanes 13**
- ☎ **91 541 72 91**
- Ⓜ **Santo Domingo**

Manuel Gonzáles Contreras
There's a waiting list for custom-built guitars, but you may find what you're looking for in Manuel Gonzáles Contrera's workshop. Classical guitarist, Andres Segovia is just one of his illustrious clients.
- ✉ **Calle Mayor 80**
- ☎ **91 542 2201**
- Ⓜ **Sol**

Septimo Arte
This shop, not far from Gran Via has a comprehensive selection of DVDs. All genres and tastes catered for.
- ✉ **Calle Hortaleza 69**
- ☎ **91 310 38 51**
- Ⓜ **Tribunal**

Food & Drink

Casa Mira
Turrón (nougat) is the national confectionery of Spain, and comes in a wide variety of flavours. This shop is owned by the descendants of a *turrón*-maker from Alicante, who brought his special recipe to Madrid in the 19th century. The mixture of almonds and honey is still made by hand.

✉ **Carrera de San Jerónimo 30**
☎ **91 429 88 95** Ⓜ **Sevilla**

Horno San Onofre
Sample the regional variety of Spanish cakes and tarts, as well as seasonal ones, traditionally made to celebrate saints' feast days. The speciality is the sponge cake-like *tarta de Santiago*.

✉ **Calle de San Onofre 2**
☎ **91 532 72 16** Ⓜ **Gran Vía**

La Mallorquina
This cake shop, which has a second branch, has been a feature of the Puerta del Sol since 1894. Locals come to buy biscuits and buns, chocolates, sweets and cakes for a special occasion.

✉ **Puerta del Sol 8/ Calle Mayor 2** ☎ **91 521 12 01**
🕐 **Mon–Sat 10–3, 5–8**
Ⓜ **Sol**

Mezquita de Estrecho
In the foyer of this mosque is a delightful grocery store, selling tubs of marinated olives, freshly-baked flat breads, spices, pastries, feta cheese and halal meat. The mosque itself welcomes visitors.

✉ **Calle Anastasio Herrero 5**
☎ **No phone** Ⓜ **Estrecho**

Museo del Jamón
This restaurant-shop is one of a chain that are hung with haunches of ham. The choice is enormous.

✉ **Calle de Alcalá 155**
☎ **91 431 72 96** Ⓜ **Atocha**

El Palacio de los Quesos
The Palace of Cheeses has all the Spanish specialities. Manchego, for example, is available *tierno* (young) to *añejo* (mature). They even have the strong-tasting *curado*, matured in oil. Try *cabrales*, a blue-veined, full-flavoured mixture of goat and sheeps' milk cheese from Asturias.

✉ **Calle Mayor 53** ☎ **91 548 16 23** Ⓜ **Sol, Opera**

Patrimonio Comunal Olivarero
In a country where olive oil is used in virtually every dish, it is not surprising to find a shop that sells nothing but *aceite de oliva virgen extra*, the best olive oil you can get.

✉ **Calle de Mejía Lequerica 1**
☎ **91 308 05 05**
Ⓜ **Alonso Martínez, Tribunal**

Reserva y Cata
This basement wine merchants in Chueca can easily be overlooked, but its selection of Spanish wines and liquers is among the best in the city.

✉ **Calle de Conde de Xiquena 13** ☎ **91 319 04 01**
Ⓜ **Colon, Banco de España**

Tutti-Frutti
An ideal refreshment stop on a hot summer's day. José Rodriguez's family business offers an exotic selection of ice creams including flavours like Philadelphia cream cheese with honey.

✉ **Cuesta de San Vicente 22**
☎ **91 541 10 74** Ⓜ **Principe Pio/Plaza de España**

What to Take Home
For a wide selection of local delicacies such as *jamón* (ham), sausages and cheese, head for the food halls at El Corte Inglés. Extra virgin olive oils are good buys. You can pick up Spanish wines and vacuum-packed foodstuffs at Barajas Airport.

Children's Attractions

Look Behind You!
The ancient art of puppetry is alive and well in Madrid. Take the children to the Parque del Retiro (► 24) on Sunday morning to see knockabout shows that produce howls of laughter and plenty of audience participation. Even if you don't speak Spanish, the language of puppetry is international. Find them by the *estanque* (lake).

As a city Madrid has a limited number of attractions that appeal to the non-Spanish-speaking child. All children, however, are welcome in cafés and restaurants, and local youngsters tend to stay up later than their contemporaries from northern Europe or America.

Aquamadrid
At San Fernando de Henares, 15km east of Madrid and open since 1987, this is a huge lake in the middle of a wooded park. The rides range from easy (Foam) to the most scary (Kamikaze), which is an 85m-long slide with a 40m drop.
✉ **Carretera Nacional II, 15.5km** ☎ **91 673 10 13** ⏰ **Jun–Sep 12–8** 🎫 **Expensive**

Aquasur
Opened in 1998 and an instant hit, this park is 40km south of the city, near Aranjuez. The most daring water slide is the Espiritubo, a steep, scary tube ride, but there are also gentler water slides for the less adventurous, a zoo, mini-golf and a huge swimming pool.
✉ **Carretera de Andalusía (N–IV) km 44** ☎ **91 891 60 34** ⏰ **Jun–Sep 11—8, 11 at weekends** ♿ **None** 🎫 **Moderate**

Aquópolis
Aquópolis claims to be the biggest aquatic park in Europe, with 17 attractions, including the 40m-high Kamikaze and the popular Tobogán Blando, with a series of harmless jumps and turns. Upgraded in 1999, the park has more trees and prettier gardens. Find it at

Villanueva de la Cañada, about 40km northwest of the city via M 503, exit 8.
✉ **Avenida de la Dehesa, Villanueva de la Cañada** ☎ **91 815 69 33** ⏰ **Jun–Sep 12–8; 11 at weekends** 🎫 **Expensive**

Faunia
The only theme park in Europe devoted to nature and biodiversity. Eight pavilions recreate different ecosystems (jungle, polar region etc), with authentic sights, sounds, smells, flora and fauna, including 3,500 animals and 1,000 plant species. Experience a tropical storm at first hand!
www.faunia.es.com
✉ **Avenida de las Comunidades 28** ☎ **91 301 62 10** ⏰ **Summer: Mon–Fri 10:30–8, Sat, Sun 10:30–9. Winter: Wed– Sun 10–6** 🚇 **Valdebernado**

IMAX Madrid
This cinema has three of the universally-popular giant format screens: IMAX, Omnimax and IMAX 3D. Films (mainly wildlife) are changed regularly, usually last about 45 minutes and run throughout the day, seven days a week. Order tickets by phone ahead of time from the central booking number: Servicaixa 902 33 22 22.
✉ **Parque Tierno Galván** ☎ **91 467 48 00** ⏰ **Daily Mon–Thu & Sun 12–1, 5–10; Sat 12–1, 5–11** 🚇 **Méndez Alvaro** 🎫 **Moderate–expensive**

Madrid Xanadu (► 115)

Parque de Atracciones
This permanent fun-fair in the Casa de Campo (► 12) has about 40 rides as well as

the usual amusements. One of the latest thrill rides is the Virtual Simulator, which has been added to others with names such as *Los Rápidos* (The Rapids), *Los Fiordos* (The Fjords) with a 15m drop and *La Máquina* (The Machine). The auditorium hosts live music concerts in the summer.

✉ **Casa de Campo** ☎ **91 463 29 00** 🕐 **Oct–Jun Mon–Fri, Sun 12–dusk, Sat 12–1AM; Jul–Sep Mon–Thu, Sun 12–1AM, Fri–Sat 12–2AM** 🚇 **Batán** 💶 **Moderate**

Parque del Retiro
There is plenty of room here for children to play, but the park is especially fun on a Sunday morning when there are puppet shows on the promenade by the lake (➤ 24).

Real Madrid
One of the world's most famous football clubs has a popular club shop, where their trademark white shirts are a best seller (➤ 44).

✉ **Paseo de la Castellana 144** ☎ **91 457 06 79** 🚇 **Santiago Bernabéu**

Safari de Madrid
Some 40km west of the city, this is a traditional safari park with elephants, giraffes, lions and tigers. There are also reptile and snake houses and, in July and August, a playground with go-karts, mini-motorbikes and a swimming-pool.

✉ **Aldea de Fresno, Carretera de Extremadura, N-V, 32km** ☎ **91 862 23 14** 🕐 **10:30–sunset** 💶 **Expensive**

Teleférico
Children love this cable-car ride (➤ 71).

Tren de la Fresa
Taking the 'Strawberry Train' down to Aranjuez (➤ 82) is a fun day out out for all ages.

The old steam train departs from Atocha Railway Station. On the journey, hostesses in period costume hand out some of the strawberries for which Aranjuez is famous. Once in the town, there is plenty of time to enjoy the gardens, riverboat rides and the royal palace

☎ **90 222 88 22** 🕐 **Apr–Jul, mid-Sep to mid-Oct. Arocha 10AM, returning 6:30PM** 💶 **Expensive**

Warnerbros Park
A great hit since it opened in 2003, this theme park on the outskirts of Madrid has five areas: Hollywood Boulevard, Cartoon Village, the Wild West Territory, Super Heroes and Warner Brothers Studios. No food or drink may be brought into the park.

www.warnerbrospark.com ✉ **San Martin de la Vega. NIV to km22, then M-506 and follow signs** ☎ **91 821 12 34** 🕐 **Apr–Jun, Sep Mon–Thu 10–8, Fri–Sun 10–midnight; Jul, Aug daily 10–midnight; Oct to mid-Nov, Fri–Sun 10–8. Closed mid-Nov to mid-Mar** 🚌 **C3 from Atocha**

Zoo Aquarium
In the Caso de Campo park, this zoo has over 2,000 animals, including snakes and tigers, plus sharks in the aquarium and a dolphinarium with two shows a day (three in summer). Their mascot Chu-lin, the giant panda died recently, but the zoo prides itself on having other rare species, such as red pandas and white tigers. The aviary has 60 birds of prey flying free. Since re-landscaping, the park looks more attractive. Small children enjoy the little train and also boat rides on the canal.

✉ **Casa de Campo** ☎ **91 512 37 70** 🕐 **10:30–dusk** 🚇 **Batán** 💶 **Expensive**

Messing About in Boats
Another amusement in the Parque del Retiro is boating on the *estanque* (lake), under the watchful eye of Alfonso XII. Across the city in the Casa de Campo (➤ 12) is another boating lake.

Bars, Clubs &
Live Music

Late Night Extra
Traffic jams at 2AM are nothing unusual during the summer in Madrid. Thousands spend the early hours chatting and drinking in *terrazas*, which spill across the pavements of the *paseos*, especially the Paseo de la Castellana.

Berlin Cabaret
Since the classy German cabaret singer Ute Lemper appeared in Madrid a few years ago, there's been no looking back. This copas bar and club, in the increasingly chic La Latina district, attracts international as well as home-grown artists.
✉ Costanilla de San Pedro 11 ☎ 91 366 20 34 🕐 Shows from 11PM daily 🚇 La Latina

Café Central
Arguably Madrid's best-known jazz café, set in a former grocery shop. The elegant decoration includes a carved wood ceiling and pictures made of leaded, coloured glass. The programme includes artists from the USA and Europe.
✉ Plaza del Angel 10 ☎ 91 369 41 43 🕐 2:30PM–2:30AM; weekends to 3:30AM 🚇 Sol

Café de Chinitas
Flamenco originated in the south of Spain, but is popular in the capital. Enthusiastic audiences are mainly Spanish, though foreigners are also fans. This restaurant, set in the basement of a 17th-century palace, has nightly shows starting at 10:30PM.
✉ Calle de Torija 7 ☎ 91 559 51 35 🕐 9PM–dawn. Closed Sun 🚇 Santo Domingo

Las Carboneras
A club run by young Flamenco enthusiasts and performers which has got rave write-ups since opening in 2002. Arrive early to get a seat.
✉ Plaza del Conde de Miranda 1 ☎ 91 542 86 77 🕐 8:30PM–2AM 🚇 Sol

Casa Patas
This popular Flamenco Club, highly regarded by locals for its classy performers, doubles as a restaurant and *tapas* bar.
✉ Calle Cañizares 10 ☎ 91 369 04 96 🕐 9PM–2AM. Closed Sun. Shows from 10:30PM Mon–Thu and 9PM–11PM and 12AM–2AM Fri–Sat 🚇 Antón Martín

Chesterfield Café
Opened in 1997, the theme here, like the name, is American, with American bands and American beer.
✉ Calle de Serrano Jover 5 ☎ 91 542 28 17 🕐 12–3:30AM. Closed Mon 🚇 Argüelles

Clamores
Although the speciality is jazz, you can expect almost any act to turn up here, including reggae, blues and Latin American folk. Shows start at 10:30PM.
✉ Calle de Alburquerque 14 ☎ 91 445 79 38 🕐 7PM–3AM 🚇 Bilbao

Fortuny
If your idea of fun is to brush shoulders with the stars, the Fortuny is one of the celebrity sanctuaries of Madrid, where Bruce Willis, Brad Pitt and others are supposed to hide from their fans. However, there is a very strict dress code at this glitzy nightclub in a converted mansion.
✉ Calle de Fortuny 34 ☎ 91 319 05 88 🕐 2PM–dawn 🚇 Rubén Darío

Garamond
In the heart of the most fashionable district of Madrid, this is one of the most fashionable discos. The main

difficulty is getting through the door; dress smartly, look affluent and you may be ushered through to see how the other half dances.

✉ **Calle Calle Garcia Luna 13** ☎ 91 416 42 74 6PM–dawn. Closed Sun, Mon ⊚ Cruz del Reyo

Los Gabrieles (€)

No point in looking for a sign; listen for the noise and you'll find it. Century-old hand-painted wall tiles depict scenes from *Don Quixote*.

✉ **Calle de Echegaray 17** ☎ 91 429 6261 ⊚ Mon–Thu 12:30PM–2AM, Fri, Sat 12:30PM–3AM ⊚ Sevilla, Sol

Houdini Club de Magia

The Spanish still enjoy a good, old-fashioned magician. This club also has a rather spooky atmosphere.

✉ **Calle de Garcia Luna 13** ☎ 91 416 42 74 ⊚ 9PM–3AM. Closed Sun, Mon ⊚ Cruz del Rayo

Joy Madrid

The lovely old Teatro Eslava (1872) has seen it all, from the old music hall shows to variety sketches. Now the three tiers of seating encircle Madrid's hottest nightclub.

✉ **Calle de Arenal 11** ☎ 91 366 37 33 ⊚ 11PM–5AM ⊚ Sol

Moby Dick

Hugely popular, hot and sweaty, this club has a varied programme of live music and DJs throughout the week.

✉ **Avenida de Brasil 5** ☎ 91 555 76 71 ⊚ 10PM–5AM. Closed Sun ⊚ Lima

Noches de Cuplé

A nostalgic night out for the older generation of Spanish,

but thoroughly enjoyed by the younger one as well. Traditional Spanish music hall entertainment with a floorshow by Olga Ramos and her daughter Olga Maria.

✉ **Calle de la Palma 51** ☎ 91 657 03 94 ⊚ 9PM–3AM ⊚ San Bernardo

Palacio Gaviria

This is not a made-up name. The handsome 19th-century mansion plays host to a variety of music in a dozen surprisingly elegant rooms. Dress code is smart, prices are justifiably high.

✉ **Calle de Arenal 9** ☎ 91 526 60 69 ⊚ 11PM–5AM ⊚ Sol

La Riviera

If you are young and love big, live rock concerts, then this is definitely the best place to go in the city.

✉ **Paseo Virgen del Puerto** ☎ 91 365 24 15 ⊚ Check listings ⊚ Puerto del Angel

Tropical House

The theme of this disco is salsa and tango. Tuesday is tango only; Sunday is devoted to Latin-American ballroom dancing.

✉ **Calle de Martín de los Heros 14** ☎ 91 541 59 37 ⊚ 11PM–dawn ⊚ Plaza de España

Villa Rosa

With its tiles on the outside and Moorish design inside, you could guess that this disco was once a flamenco club. There are still flamenco nights as well as salsa nights, but most of the time it's a busy disco.

✉ **Plaza de Santa Ana 15** ☎ 91 521 36 89 ⊚ 11PM–dawn. Closed Sun ⊚ Sol

Gay Madrid

Madrid has the second biggest gay community in Europe, centred on the Chueca district, just north of the Gran Vía. In the small squares and narrow streets are bars, shops, discotheques and some of the best new restaurants in the city. The atmosphere is relaxed, with gays, lesbians and the straight community mixing (⊚ Chueca).

Theatre, Cinema, Music & Dance

What's Up?
When it comes to entertainment, Madrid has several weekly guides to what is on in the city. Free, pocket-sized bi-lingual magazines such as the tourist board's *En Madrid What's On* and *Lo Mejor de Madrid* (*The Best of Madrid*) give the highlights for international visitors. By far the most comprehensive listings are in the 180-page *Guía del Ocio* (*Leisure Guide*), which has every event, major and minor, but this is only in Spanish. Also look out for the monthly newspaper, *In Madrid*, with articles and listings aimed specially at young people.

Casa de América
This cultural centre dedicated to things Latin American (➤ 34) has daily presentations of film, plays and music.

☒ Paseo de Recoletos 2
☎ 91 595 48 00 ◷ Tue–Sat 11–2, 5–8; Sun & festivals 11–2
🚇 Banco de España

Centro Cultural Conde Duque
This cultural centre (➤ 38) has a busy programme year round, but it is at its best in the summer (mid-Jun to mid-Sep) when the courtyard is taken over by the Veranos de la Villa, a summer festival of jazz, classical music, ballet and opera. Several other sites in the city also take part in this festival.

☒ Calle de Conde Duque 11
☎ 91 588 58 34 ◷ Box office: 10:30–2, 5:30–9. Closed Mon 🚇 Ventura Rodríguez, Noviciado, San Bernardo

Centro Cultural de la Villa
There are plans to rebuild this modern cultural centre, currently situated underground, behind the waterfall of the Plaza Colón. As the city's official cultural centre, it stages a wide variety of performances year round, but is particularly known for *zarzuela* (light opera) and dance.

☒ Plaza de Colón ☎ 91 480 03 00 ◷ Box office: 11–1:30, 5–6. Closed Mon 🚇 Colón

Círculo de las Bellas Artas
This arts complex has a small but attractive theatre, as well as a library and café.

☒ Calle del Marqués de Casa Riera 2 ☎ 91 532 44 37
🚇 Banco de España ◷ Box office: Tue–Sun 11:30–1:30

Teatro Monumental
This auditorium is the home of the orchestra of Spain's national television station. The season runs from October to April. In addition to the well-priced concerts, there are performances of *zarzuela* and opera.

☒ Calle de Atocha 65
☎ 91 429 12 81 ◷ Box office: Sep–Jun daily 11–2, 5–9; Jul Mon–Fri 9–2 🚇 Antón Martín

Teatro Real
The 1990s saw this theatre restored to its 1850s grandeur and it has now joined the ranks of Europe's great opera houses. The season runs from September to July, and since opera is very popular, tickets can be difficult to come by. There are regular backstage tours (Tuesday–Friday at 10:30, 11:30 and 12:30).

☒ Plaza de Oriente ☎ 91 516 06 60 ◷ Box office 10–1:30, 5:30–8. Closed Sun. Tickets also from www.entradas.com 🚇 Opera

Teatro de la Zarzuela
Zarzuela is the light opera of Spain and Madrid is considered its home. Spanish light opera may not get the recognition that serious opera receives, but it is worth noting that Plácido Domingo, whose parents were *zarzuela* singers, has recorded popular songs in this style. The theatre was built in 1856 and is a copy of La Scala in Milan.

☒ Calle de Jovellanos 4
☎ 91 524 54 10 ◷ Box office 12–6. Tickets also from www.entrades.com
🚇 Banco de España

Sport

Spectator Sports

Basketball

Real Madrid's basketball team has a record that was, until recently, almost as dazzling as the football squad. Real play in the Palacio Raimundo Saporta from Sep to May.

✉ Paseo de la Castellana 259
☎ 902 2817 09 ⏰ Box office: 11–2, 5–8 🚇 Goya

Football

For Real Madrid details (▶ 44, 111).
Perennial rivals of Real Madrid, Atlético Madrid play in a 60,000-seat stadium. Since returning to the first division in 2002, they have been attempting to recapture the form of 1996 when they won the league and cup.

✉ Estadio Vicente Calderón
☎ 91 366 47 07 ⏰ Box office: 5–8. Closed Sat, Sun
🚇 Pirámides

Participatory Sports

Golf

With the success of Seve Ballesteros and José María Olazábal, golf is enjoying a boom in Spain. Although it can be an expensive pasttime, there is a good choice of 18-hole golf courses around Madrid.

Club de Campo Villa de Madrid
✉ Carretera de Castilla, 2km
☎ 91 550 08 40 🚌 84

Ice-skating

You can hire ice-skates and helmets at the indoor Sport Hielo.

✉ Estación de Chamartín
☎ 91 315 63 08 ⏰ Thu 5:30–9:30, Fri 5:30–10; Sat, Sun

11:30–2PM, 5:30–10.30. Closed Jun, Jul, Aug 🚇 Chamartín

Dream Palacio de Hielo
The ice rink is just one feature of this sports and leisure complex which has a swimming pool, solarium, gym, bowling alley, cinema, shops and restaurants.

✉ Calle Silvano 77, Canillas
☎ 91 716 01 59 ⏰ Tue–Thu 8:45–10:15, Fri, Sat 12–3, 4:30–midnight, Sun 12–3, 4:30–10. Closed Mon
🚇 Esperanza

Skiing

At weekends skiers head for the mountains north of the city, an hour or so away by car. Resorts include:
Navacerrada ☎ 91 852 1435,
La Pinilla ☎ 92 155 03 04,
Valcotos ☎ 91 563 30 61

Xanadu

The large indoor ski slope is the centrepiece of this vast new shopping and entertainment complex. Slopes for novices and professionals, a ski school and equipment rental.

✉ Carratera NV km 23 Arroyomolinos ☎ 902 26 30 26 ⏰ All year. Sun–Thu 10–2AM, 10–4AM Fri, Sat 🚌 528 from Príncipe Pío

Swimming

There are several open-air pools run by the city. In the Casa de Campo, there is one for children, one intermediate and one of Olympic size. All are busy on summer weekends. See also Aquamadrid, Aquasur and Aquópolis (▶ 110).

✉ Casa de Campo, Avenida del Angel ☎ 91 463 00 50 ⏰ Early Jun–Sep 10:30–8 🚇 Largo

Bullfighting

Opinions differ on the role of bullfighting. Is it a sport, an art form or an integral part of Spain's national identity? The decision is very individual. In recent years, *corridas* (fights) have drawn ever-more enthusiastic crowds to the Plaza de Toros of Las Ventas, the world's most famous arena, in the east of the city (▶ 63).

What's On When

San Isidro

Although the feast day of San Isidro, Madrid's patron saint, is on 15 May, the festival lasts for three weeks. After mass on 15 May, a pilgrimage crosses the Río Manzanares, and locals in traditional dress drink water from a fountain (which has been blessed), picnic on *rosquillas* (sweet buns) and dance. Theatre, concerts and 28 bullfights, rated the world's most prestigious, are all part of the festivities.

January

Cabalgata de los Reyes Magos (5 Jan): the evening procession of the Three Kings leads on to the next day's *Epifania* (Epiphany), when the kings throw sweets to children lining the streets.

February

ARCO (Feb): Contemporary Art Fair, a leading event for top artists, dealers and collectors from all over the world, although it is less successful now than it has been in the past.
Carnaval: before Lent, Madrid parties. A ceremony called the *Entierro de la Sardina* (the Burial of the Sardine), takes place in the Casa del Campo (➤ 12).

March/April

Semana Santa (Holy Week): celebrated with solemn processions of penitents through the streets.

May

Dos de Mayo (2 May): Madrid remembers the day when *madrileños* rose up against the French in 1808.
Festimad (early May): once an 'alternative' festival but now big business right across the spectrum – films, poetry readings, music, dance and more in the Bellas Artes building and in Móstoles, in the suburbs.
San Isidro (15 May): Madrid's patron saint.
Feria del Libro (the Festival of the Book): held in the Parque del Retiro where booksellers set up hundreds of stalls (➤ 24).

June

San Antonio de la Florida (13 Jun): At the Ermita de San Antonio de la Florída, unmarried girls visit the chapel to make them lucky in love (➤ 39).
San Juan (17–24 Jun): fireworks in the Parque del Retiro to celebrate the festival of St John (➤ 24).
Los Veranos de la Villa (Jun–Sep): a season of music, theatre, *zarzuela*, dance and open-air cinema, put on under the auspices of the Villa de Madrid; the main venue is the Conde-Duque cultural centre.

July

Virgen del Carmen (16 Jul): local festivals for the Virgin in the suburbs of Chamberí, Villaverde and Vallecas.

August

San Cayetano, San Lorenzo (10 Aug), the *Virgen de la Paloma* (15 Aug): local *fiestas* in La Latina, Argumosa and Lavapiés.

October/November

Festival de Otoño: a festival involving all the performing arts based round a theme, for example a country or literary figure.

November

Fiesta de la Almudena (9 Nov): festival of the (female) patron saint of Madrid.

December

Feria de Artesania (Dec–6 Jan): Advent craft fair centred on the Paseo de Recoletos (➤ 59).
Nochevieja (New Year's Eve): thousands of people fill the Puerta del Sol to watch the clock and follow the tradition of swallowing one grape at each of the 12 strokes of midnight.

Practical Matters

Above: *Metro entrance,
Puerta del Sol*
Right: *it's good
to talk*

TIME DIFFERENCES

GMT 12 noon	Madrid → 1PM	Germany → 1PM	USA (NY) ← 7AM	Netherlands → 1PM	France → 1PM

BEFORE YOU GO

WHAT YOU NEED

● Required ○ Suggested ▲ Not required	Some countries require a passport to remain valid for a minimum period (usually at least six months) beyond the date of entry – contact their consulate or embassy or your travel agent for details.	UK	Germany	USA	Netherlands
Passport		●	●	●	●
Visa (regulations can change – check before booking your trip)		▲	▲	▲	▲
Onward or Return Ticket		▲	▲	●	▲
Health Inoculations		▲	▲	▲	▲
Health Documentation (► 123, Health)		●	●	●	●
Travel Insurance		○	○	○	○
Driving Licence (national with Spanish translation or International)		●	●	●	●
Car Insurance Certificate (if own car)		●	●	●	●
Car Registration Document (if own car)		●	●	●	●

WHEN TO GO

Madrid

High season

Low season

9°C	11°C	15°C	18°C	21°C	27°C	31°C	30°C	25°C	19°C	13°C	9°C
JAN	FEB	MAR	APR	MAY	JUN	JUL	AUG	SEP	OCT	NOV	DEC

Very wet   Wet   Cloud   Sun   Sun/showers

TOURIST OFFICES

In the UK
Spanish Tourist Office
79 New Cavendish Street
London
W1W 6XB
☎ 020 7486 8077
Fax: 020 7486 8034
www.spain.info

In the USA
Tourist Office of Spain
666 Fifth Avenue
(35th Floor)
New York, NY 10103
☎ (212) 265 8822
Fax: (212) 265 8864
www.okspain.org

Tourist Office of Spain
8383 Wilshire Boulevard
Suite 960
Beverley Hills
CA 90211
☎ (213) 658 7192
Fax: (213) 658 1061

EMERGENCY 112

POLICE 091 (National), 092 (Madrid)

FIRE 080

AMBULANCE 061, RED CROSS 91 522 22 22

WHEN YOU ARE THERE

ARRIVING

Aeropuerto de Barajas, east of the city, has three terminals: T-1 for international flights; T-2 for national and as well as some Iberia flights within Europe, and T-3 for regional flights and the Madrid-Barcelona shuttle. General enquiries ☎ 91 393 60 00. Flight information ☎ 91 305 83 43. In 1999 a metro link with the city was opened. Madrid is served by the world's major airlines.

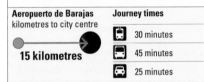

Aeropuerto de Barajas kilometres to city centre	Journey times
15 kilometres	🚇 30 minutes
	🚌 45 minutes
	🚕 25 minutes

MONEY

Since 1 January 2002, the peseta has given way to the euro, which is divided into 100 cents (or *centesimi*). Coins come in denominations of 1, 2, 5, 10, 20 and 50 cents, 1 and 2 euros, and notes come in 5, 10, 20, 50, 100, 200 and 500 euro denominations (the last two are rarely seen). The notes and one side of the coins are the same throughout the European single currency zone, but each country has a different design on one face of each of the coins. Notes and coins from any of the other countries can be used in Spain.

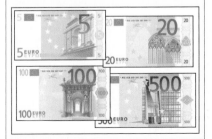

TIME

 Madrid is on CET (Central European Time), one hour ahead of GMT (Greenwich Mean Time). Summer time starts on the last Sunday in March and ends on the last Sunday of October.

CUSTOMS

➡ **YES**

From another EU country for personal use (guidelines):
800 cigarettes, 200 cigars, 1 kilogram of tobacco
10 litres of spirits (over 22%)
20 litres of aperitifs
90 litres of wine, of which 60 litres can be sparkling wine
110 litres of beer

From a non-EU country the allowances are:
200 cigarettes OR 50 cigars OR 250 grams of tobacco
1 litre of spirits (over 22%)
2 litres of fortified wine (eg sherry), sparkling wine or other liqueurs
2 litres of still wine
50 ml of perfume
250ml of eau de toilette
Travellers under 17 are not entitled to the tobacco and alcohol allowances.

 NO

Drugs, firearms, ammunition, offensive weapons, obscene material, unlicensed animals.

CONSULATES

UK
91 308 52 01

USA
91 587 22 00

Germany
91 557 90 00

Netherlands
91 353 75 00

France
91 700 78 00

WHEN YOU ARE THERE

TOURIST OFFICES

Tourist and Cultural information Line
☎ 010 (91 366 66 04 outside Madrid)

Oficina Municipal de Turismo
● Plaza Mayor 3
☎ 91 366 54 77

Oficinas de Información Turística de la Communidad de Madrid
● Calle Duque de Medinaceli 2
☎ 91 429 49 51

Also at
Puerta de Toledo Market
● Stand 3134
☎ 91 364 18 76

Estación de Chamartín
● Chamartín Railway Station
☎ 91 315 99 76

Barajas Airport
● T-1 Terminal (international arrivals)
☎ 91 305 86 56

Madrid Tourist Information website: munimadrid.es

NATIONAL HOLIDAYS

J	F	M	A	M	J	J	A	S	O	N	D
2		1	1	3			1			1	2	3

1 Jan	Año Nuevo (New Year's Day)
6 Jan	Reyes (Three Kings)
Mar/Apr	Jueves Santo, Viernes Santo (Easter Thursday, Good Friday)
1 May	Fiesta del Trabajo (May Day)
2 May	Día de la Comunidad (Madrid Day)
15 May	San Isidro (Madrid's patron saint)
15 Aug	Virgen de la Paloma (Assumption)
12 Oct	Día de la Hispanidad (Discovery of America Day)
1 Nov	Todos los Santos (All Saints' Day)
9 Nov	Virgen de la Almudena
6 Dec	Día de la Constitución (Constitution Day)
8 Dec	La Inmaculada (Immaculate Conception)
25 Dec	Navidad (Christmas)

OPENING HOURS

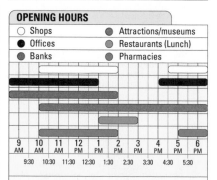

○ Shops ● Attractions/museums
● Offices ● Restaurants (Lunch)
● Banks ● Pharmacies

Major museums are open all day, but close on Monday or Tuesday. Smaller museums close for lunch. Shops vary, with most open Monday to Saturday. Some close Saturday afternoon, and most close all day Sunday. Department stores and malls are open 10–9. Many restaurants and shops close during August. During the San Isidro festival in May, banks close at noon. In July and August many offices work straight through from 8 to 3, then close. Apart from opening for mass, well-known churches have set opening hours.

DRIVE ON THE
RIGHT

TOILETS
FREE

★ ★
★ ★

PUBLIC TRANSPORT

 Internal Flights
Iberia, the national carrier, has regular flights linking Madrid with other major cities in Spain. The most frequent are between Madrid and Barcelona, with the *Puente Aéreo* (shuttle service) operating from 7AM–11PM.

 Trains
The main office of RENFE (Spanish National Railways) is at Calle de Alcalá 44. Tickets and information are also available at Barajas Airport and the three main stations. From Atocha, trains are mainly to southern Spain. The AVE high-speed service to Seville leaves from Puerta de Atocha. From Chamartín, trains go to the north, northeast and France. Travellers can get discounts on some journeys if they travel on so-called 'blue days', marked on calendars available from any RENFE office. A special card for tourists gives unlimited travel on the system.

 Buses
Estación Sur de Autobuses, the city's main bus station, is at the corner of Calle Méndez Alvaro and Calle Retama. Near by are the Atocha Railway Station and Méndez Alvaro Metro station. Although buses cover the whole of Madrid, the system is somewhat complicated to understand and it is easier to take the Metro.

 Metro
The easiest way to get around Madrid, apart from on foot, is by Metro. The 11-line, colour-coded system has stops close to all the major attractions. The direction of the train is shown by the name of the terminus station. Trains run 6AM–1:30AM. Fares are inexpensive. If you buy a *bono de diez viajes*, (10-ride ticket for Metro or bus), you get a discount.

CAR RENTAL

 As usual in large airports, all the major car rental companies are represented at Barajas Airport. They also have offices in the middle of Madrid, but you could choose to rent from a local agency. The minimum age for hiring a car is 21.

TAXIS

  Official taxis are white with a diagonal red stripe. Look for the *libre* (free) sign behind the windscreen or a green light on top of the cab. Fares are reasonable. Make sure the meter is not running when you get in. Travel from the airport costs extra.

DRIVING

 Speed limit on motorways: **120kph**

 Speed limit on main roads: **100kph**

 Speed limit on minor roads: **90kph** urban roads: **50kph**

 Seat belts must be worn in front seats and rear seats where fitted.

 Penalties are heavy for driving under the influence of alcohol or drugs. It is compulsory to take drink/drug tests when requested by police. Failure to comply is a serious offence.

Regulations It is illegal to drive while wearing headphones or using hand-held mobile phones.

Fines for traffic offences are stringent and payment is required on the spot.

 Lead-free petrol (*sin plomo*) is readily available. Other types include *super* (4 star), *normal* (3 star) and *gasoleo* (diesel).

 Drivers must carry two warning triangles, spare bulbs and fuses, a spare wheel and a fluorescent jacket. The towing of motor vehicles is not permitted, except to move a broken-down car out of traffic or to a safe place. Only a breakdown vehicle is allowed to tow a broken-down car.

PERSONAL SAFETY

As in most big cities, pickpockets are a problem in Madrid, especially in busy places such as open-air markets, large shops and railway stations. Valuables such as tickets and passports should be locked up in the hotel rather than carried with you. The Rastro Flea Market is a place where you need to be particularly careful. Madrid is a late-night city, but stay on main streets where there are more people. Be sure to take official taxis only (➤ 121).

City Police
☎ **092**
Emergency
☎ **112**

ELECTRICITY

The power supply in Madrid is 220 volts AC; sockets have two-pin plugs. If you have a British appliance, you will need an adaptor; North American appliances also require a transformer.

TELEPHONES

There are plenty of telephone booths in the streets. Local calls are inexpensive. Although you can pay with coins, it is quicker and easier to buy a phonecard from any *tabaco* (tobacconist). Many phones also take credit cards. Long-distance calls

are cheaper from a booth than from your hotel. Directory information is 003.

International Dialling Codes
From Madrid to:

UK:	**00 44**
Germany:	**00 49**
USA and Canada:	**00 1**
Netherlands:	**00 31**
France:	**00 33**

POST

The main post office, the Palacio de Comunicaciones, is on the Plaza de la Cibeles, open Mon–Fri 8AM–9:30PM, Sat 8:30–2:30. Elsewhere, *correos* (post offices) are open Mon–Sat 9–2. Stamps (*sellos*) are also sold in any *tabaco*, the tobacconist shop identified by the brown and yellow sign. To post a letter, look for yellow post boxes.

TIPS/GRATUITIES

Yes ✓ No ✗		
Restaurants	✓	5–10%
Cafés/bars (if service not included)	✓	5%
Tour guides	✓	€1
Hairdressers	✓	5%
Taxis	✓	5%
Chambermaids	✓	€1
Porters (per bag)	✓	€1
Theatre/cinema usherettes	✓	€1
Cloakroom attendants	✓	€1
Toilets	✗	no

PHOTOGRAPHY

What to photograph: The narrow streets in old Madrid, grand buildings and the Parque del Retiro. The Cibeles fountain with the post office behind is a classic Madrid scene.

When to photograph: Morning and late afternoon are best since the strong midday sun flattens perspective and washes out colours.

Where to buy film: Branches of VIPs shops and Corte Inglés (department stores) carry a wide range of film and camera batteries.

HEALTH

Doctors
EU nationals can get medical treatment in Spain with the relevant documentation (Form E111 for Britons), although private medical insurance is still advised and is essential for all other visitors. US visitors should check their insurance coverage. English-speaking doctors are available at the Anglo-American Medical Unit ☎ 91 435 18 23.

Dental Services
EU citizens are not covered by the E111 form for the cost of seeing a dentist. All visitors have to pay the full price of a visit and any treatment. Ask at your hotel's reception desk for advice on the nearest dentist.

Sun Advice
Madrid is at a high altitude and has a dry climate and strong sun, so use sunscreen in spring and autumn, as well as in high summer. Hats and sunglasses also give useful protection.

Drugs
Prescription and non-prescription drugs are sold in *farmacias* (chemists), identified by a green cross. In central Madrid, the Farmacia Goya 89 ☎ 91 435 49 58 and the Farmacia Lastra ☎ 91 402 42 72 are open 24 hours a day. If you are on medication, carry photocopies of the prescription.

Safe Water
Madrid is famous for the quality of its drinking water and, unlike many other Spanish cities, it does not have the taste of chlorine. Locals are always aware of the need to conserve water. In bathrooms, the hot tap is labelled 'c' for *caliente*, the cold has 'f' for *frío*.

CONCESSIONS

Concessions Many museums offer free admission to the general public, or citizens of the EU on certain days, or during certain hours. It is important to have a passport or national identity card if you are going to claim a concession.

Senior Citizens The over-65s can gain free entry to many museums and galleries.

Students Reductions are available for students in many museums on production of an ISIC (international student identity card.)

Under-18s The under-18s can gain free entry to many museums and galleries.

CLOTHING SIZES

Spain	UK	Rest of Europe	USA	
46	36	46	36	
48	38	48	38	
50	40	50	40	
52	42	52	42	Suits
54	44	54	44	
56	46	56	46	
41	7	41	8	
42	7½	42	9	
43	8½	43	10	
44	9½	44	11	Shoes
45	10½	45	12	
46	11	46	13	
37	14½	37	14½	
38	15	38	15	
39/40	15½	39/40	15½	
41	16	41	16	Shirts
42	16½	42	16.5	
43	17	43	17	
36	8	36	6	
38	10	38	8	
40	12	40	10	
42	14	42	12	Dresses
44	16	44	14	
46	18	46	16	
38	4½	38	6	
38	5	38	6½	
39	5½	39	7	
39	6	39	7½	Shoes
40	6½	40	8	
41	7	41	8½	

WHEN DEPARTING

- Check the time of your return flight the day before departure. In 1999 Line 8 was extended to the airport, which now has its own Metro station. But, whether getting to the airport by car or Metro, allow extra time if you are travelling during the morning or afternoon rush hours.

LANGUAGE

The Spanish are pleased when foreigners try to speak their language. Don't worry about making mistakes; although they will correct them, it is always with a smile, and a sincere attempt to understand what you are trying to communicate. English is the most commonly taught foreign language; the younger generation usually know a little and often quite a lot. Although pamphlets in foreign languages are available in the larger museums, signs and guided tours in foreign languages are rare.

accommodation	alojamiento	room service	servicio de
hotel	hotel		habitaciones
bed and	pensión	chambermaid	camarera
breakfast		bath	baño
single room	habitación	shower	ducha
	individual	toilet	servicio
double room	habitación doble	balcony	balcón
one person	una persona	key	llave
one night	una noche	quiet room	habitación
reservation	reserva		tranquila
lift	ascensor		

bank	banco	travellers'	cheque de
exchange office	cambio	cheque	viaje
post office	correos	credit card	tarjeta de
coin	moneda		credito
banknote	billete	exchange rate	cambio
cheque	cheque	commission	comisión
change	cambio	charge	

café	cafetería	starter	primer plato
pub/bar	bar	main course	secundo plato
breakfast	desayuno	dessert	postre
lunch	almuerzo	bill	cuenta
dinner	cena	beer	cerveza
table	mesa	wine	vino
waiter	camarero	water	agua
waitress	camerera	coffee	café

aeroplane	avión	single ticket	billete de ida
airport	aeropuerto	return ticket	billete de ida y
train	tren		vuelta
bus	autobús	non-smoking	no fumador
station	estación	car	coche
boat	barca	petrol	gasolina
port	puerto	bus stop	parada
ticket	billete	where is...?	¿donde está...?

yes	sí	excuse me	por favor
no	no	you're welcome	de nada
please	por favor	how are you?	¿ qué tal?
thank you	graçias	do you speak	¿ habla inglés?
welcome	bienvenido	English?	
hello	hola	I don't under-	no entiendo
goodbye	adios	stand	
good morning	buenos días	how much?	¿ cuánto es?
good afternoon	buenas tardes	open	abierto
goodnight	buenas noches	closed	cerrado

INDEX

Acknowledgements

The Automobile Association would like to thank the following photographers, liibraries and museums for their assistance in the preparation of this book

ANDALUCIA SLIDE LIBRARY 9b, 65, 79, 117b, 122a, 122c;
BRIDGEMAN ART LIBRARY The Spinners, or The Fable of Arachne, c.1657 (oil on canvas) by Diego Rodriguez de Silva y Velasquez (1599–1660), Prado, Madrid, Spain/Peter Willi/Bridgeman Art Library 26b; MARY EVANS PICTURE LIBRARY 10b, 11b, 11c; MUSEO DE AMÉRICA (MADRID) 17b, 17c; REX FEATURES 14b; SPECTRUM COLOUR LIBRARY 85b, 86b; WORLD PICTURES 2, 8b, 82b; www.euro.ecb.int 119 (euro notes).

The remaining photographs are held in the Association's own library (AA PHOTOLIBRARY) and were taken by Michelle Chaplow, with the exception of 49, 50b, 51b, 61a, 68/69, 76, 77, 78, 80, 81, 82a, 83a, 83b, 85a, 86a, 87a, 87b, 88a, 88b, 88c, 89a, 89b, 90a which were taken by J Edmanson; 84, 85c, 90b were taken by Philip Enticknap; 29, 44b, 61a were taken by Max Jourdan; 5a, 6a, 6c, 7a, 7b, 8a, 10a, 11a, 12a, 13a, 14a, 18b, 20b, 20/21, 21b, 22b, 27a, 27b, 28a, 28/29, 29a, 30, 32a, 33a, 34a, 34b, 36a, 36c, 38a, 39a, 40, 41, 42, 43a, 44a, 46, 47a, 48a, 50a, 51a, 52, 53a, 53b, 54, 55a, 56a, 57a, 57b, 59, 60a, 66, 67, 69a, 69b, 70a, 71a, 72a, 73, 74a, 75a, 91a, 92, 93, 94, 95, 96, 97, 98, 99, 100, 101, 102, 103, 104, 105, 106, 107, 108, 109, 110, 111, 112, 113, 114, 115, 116, 117a were taken by Rick Strange.

Copy editor: Sally MacEachern   Page layout: Barfoot Design
Revision management: Pam Stagg

Dear Essential Traveller

Your comments, opinions and recommendations are very important to us. So please help us to improve our travel guides by taking a few minutes to complete this simple questionnaire.

You do not need a stamp (unless posted outside the UK). If you do not want to cut this page from your guide, then photocopy it or write your answers on a plain sheet of paper.

Send to: **The Editor, AA World Travel Guides, FREEPOST SCE 4598, Basingstoke RG21 4GY.**

Your recommendations...

We always encourage readers' recommendations for restaurants, nightlife or shopping – if your recommendation is used in the next edition of the guide, we will send you a **FREE** AA *Essential* **Guide** of your choice. Please state below the establishment name, location and your reasons for recommending it.

_____

_____

_____

_____

Please send me **AA *Essential*** _____

About this guide...

Which title did you buy?

AA *Essential* _____

Where did you buy it? _____

When? m m / y y

Why did you choose an AA *Essential* Guide? _____

_____

_____

_____

_____

Did this guide meet your expectations?

Exceeded ☐ Met all ☐ Met most ☐ Fell below ☐

Please give your reasons _____

_____

_____

_____

continued on next page...

Were there any aspects of this guide that you particularly liked? _____

_____

_____

Is there anything we could have done better? _____

_____

_____

About you...

Name (*Mr/Mrs/Ms*) _____

    Address _____

_____

_____ Postcode _____

    Daytime tel nos _____

Please only give us your mobile phone number if you wish to hear from us about other products and services from the AA and partners by text or mms.

Which age group are you in?

    Under 25 ☐   25–34 ☐   35–44 ☐   45–54 ☐   55–64 ☐   65+ ☐

How many trips do you make a year?

    Less than one ☐   One ☐   Two ☐   Three or more ☐

Are you an AA member? Yes ☐   No ☐

About your trip...

When did you book? m m / y y   When did you travel? m m / y y

How long did you stay? _____

Was it for business or leisure? _____

Did you buy any other travel guides for your trip?

    If yes, which ones? _____

Thank you for taking the time to complete this questionnaire. Please send it to us as soon as possible, and remember, you do not need a stamp (*unless posted outside the UK*).

Happy Holidays!

The Atlas

Acknowledgements
All pictures are from AA World Travel Library with contributions from the following photographers:
Max Jourdan: Corral de la Morrie flamenco show; musicians performing at Corral de la Morrie
flamenco show, Cibeles fountain in Plaza de la Cibeles, boys playing football
T Oliver: fringed banner at Palacio Real

www.theAA.com
The Automobile Association's website offers comprehensive and up-to-the-minute information covering AA-approved hotels, guest houses and B&Bs, restaurants and pubs in the UK; airport parking, insurance, European breakdown cover, European motoring advice, a ferry planner, European route planner, overseas fuel prices, a bookshop and much more.

www.aaa.com
AAA's website offers comprehensive information covering AAA-approved hotels and restaurants in the US. In addition, AAA can assist US citizens with obtaining a passport, reservations and tickets for cruise, tour, motorcoach, rail and air travel. AAA provides information on independent or escorted tours for individuals or groups and offers benefits on cruises, tours and travel packages.

The Foreign and Commonwealth Office Country advice, traveller's tips, before you go information, checklists and more.
www.fco.gov.uk

Spanish National Tourist Office
www.tourspain.co.uk

GENERAL
UK Passport Service
www.ukpa.gov.uk

US passport information .
www.travel.state.gov

Health Advice for Travellers
www.doh.gov.uk/traveladvice

The Full Universal Currency Converter
www.xe.com/ucc/full.shtml

Flying with Kids
www.flyingwithkids.com

Information about the capital's main museums. It's in Spanish but is useful to consult for special exhibitions, changes in opening times etc.
www.cultura.mecd.es/museos/

What's on, maps and street plans, flight information, exhibition guide, restaurant tips, rural tourism, suggestions for walks.
www.descubremadrid.com

Good site for researching your trip and getting the most out of your visit.
www.thingstodo-madrid.com/

Click on 'Madrid' for the capital's number one listing magazine. It's in Spanish and is the cultural bible for Madrileños.
www.guiadelocio.com

Firm offering car tours out of town and guided walks around major sights like the Monasterio de las Descalzas Reales.
www.easygoin.org

Comprehensive site produced by an adopted Madrileño of 15 years' standing.
www.GoMadrid.com

Online booking service with a wide selection of accommodation in Madrid.
www.hotelconnect.co.uk

Useful site about Spain and Madrid: what's on, sightseeing, hotels, travel tips – ideal for consulting before you go.
www.madridbyclick.com/madrid

The Madrid Tourist Board offers an online hotel reservation service, with last-minute availability and discounted rates.
www.madridtourism.org/

TRAVEL
www.worldairportguide.com

Information about Barajas airport.
www.madrid-mad.com

Details of public transport – fares, schedules for the metro, bus and local train networks.
www.ctm-madrid.es

Motorway Autobahn		Autoroute Autopista, autovía
Main road Hauptstraße		Route principale Carretera principal
Other roads Sonstige Straßen		Autres routes Otras carreteras
Pedestrian precinct Fußgängerzone		Zone piétonne Zona peatonal
Main line railway Fernverkehrsbahn		Chemin de fer: ligne à grand traffic Línea principal de ferrocarril
Secondary line railway Sonstige Eisenbahn		Chemin de fer: ligne à traffic secondaire Línea secundaria de ferrocarril
Aerial cableway Seilbahn		Téléférique Teleférico
Underground with station Untergrundbahn mit Haltestelle		Métro avec station Metro con estación
Underground under construction Untergrundbahn in Bau		Métro en construction Metro en construcción
Public or notable building Öffentliches oder bemerkenswertes Gebäude		Édifice public ou remarquable Edificio público o notable
Information • Post office Information • Postamt	ⓘ ✉	Informations • Poste Oficina de información • Oficina de correo
Museum • Monument Museum • Denkmal	M̂ ⚊	Musée • Monument Museo • Monumento
Hospital Krankenhaus	⊞	Hôpital Hospital
Police Polizei	✲	Police Policía
Car park Parkplatz	P	Parking Aparcamiento
Church Kirche	†	Église Iglesia
Synagogue Synagoge	✡	Synagogue Sinagoga
Mosque Moschee	C	Mosquée Mezquita

134-145	0 — 200 m 0 — 200 yards
146-147	0 — 5 km 0 — 3 miles

Maps © Mairs Geographischer Verlag / Falk Verlag, 73751 Ostfildern

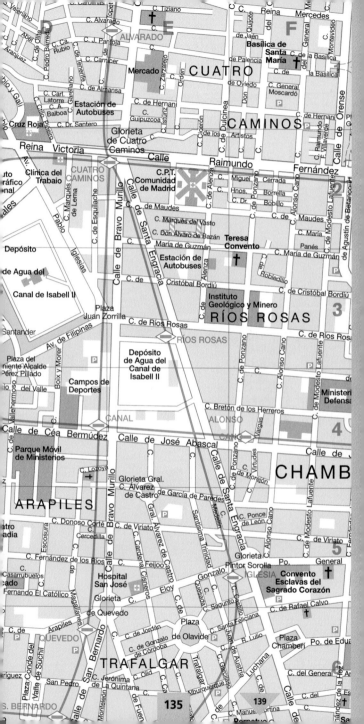

C. de Carolinas
C. Tiziano
Reina Mercedes
Montevideo
C. Valeriano
C. Alvarado
Quijote
del
F
C. Abel
C. de Oliva
C. J. Pantoja
ALVARADO
de Jaén
Basílica de
Santa
María
C. de la Basílica
C. Pedro Barreda
C. Rubio
C. Carnicer
Odén
C. de Palencia
C. de la Basílica
Aranjuez
C. de Tenerife
C. Zurzarejo
CUATRO
C. Carl. Latorre
C. de Almansa
Mercado
de Oviedo
C. General Moscardó
C.A. Balboa
Galeano
C. de Hernani
CAMINOS
C. Cicerón
C. de Hernani
de Orense
Cruz Roja
C. Dr. Santero
C. Guipúzcoa
de los
Artistas
Calle
Glorieta
de Cuatro
Caminos
Reina Victoria
Calle
Raimundo
Fernández
Clínica del
Trabajo
CUATRO
CAMINOS
C.P.T.
Comunidad
de Madrid
C. de Alenza
Miguel
Cerrada
C. de Ponzano
2
de Maudes
Hnos.
Borrella
Maudes
C. Marqués del Vasto
C. María
C. Don Álvaro de Bazán
Teresa
Convento
Panés
Depósito
María de Guzmán
C. de
María de Guzmán
de Agua del
Estación de
Autobuses
Robledillo
Canal de Isabell II
C. de Cristóbal Bordiú
C. de
Cristóbal Bordiú
Instituto
Geológico y Minero
RÍOS ROSAS
3
Plaza
Juan Zorrilla
C. de Ríos Rosas
C. de Ríos Rosas
Santander
RÍOS ROSAS
Depósito
de Agua del
Canal de
Isabell II
C. de Ponzano
Plaza del
niente Alcalde
Pérez Pillado
Campos de
Deportes
Ministerio
Defensa
CANAL
C. Bretón de los Herreros
ALONSO
Calle de Céa Bermúdez
Calle de José Abascal
Calle de
4
Parque Móvil
de Ministerios
CHAMB
C. Lozoya
Glorieta Gral.
C. Álvarez
de Castro
de García de Parades
de Morijón
C. de Virtudes
ARAPILES
C. Donoso Corté
C. de Viriato
C. Ponce
de León
de Viriato
Cercedilla
5
C. Fernández de los Ríos
Glorieta
Pintor Sorolla
Po.
General
Hospital
San José
IGLESIA
Convento
Esclavas del
Sagrado Corazón
Glorieta
de Quevedo
C. de Rafael Calvo
C. de Jordán
Plaza
Chamberí
Po. de Edua
QUEVEDO
C. de Gonzalo
de Córdoba
Plaza de Olavide
Luchana
C. del General
TRAFALGAR
C. Jerónima
de la Quintana
C. Olid
S. BERNARDO
San Pedro
135
139

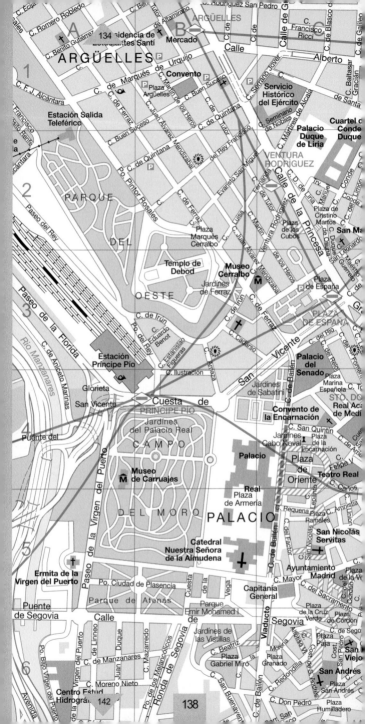

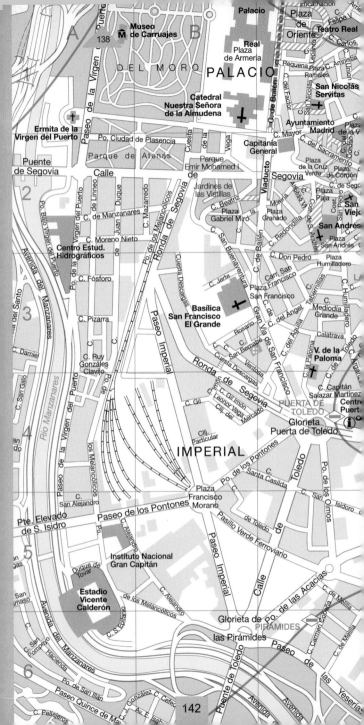

A

B

Puerto

Paseo de la Virgen

Museo M de Carruajes

DEL MORO

Palacio

Real Plaza de Armeria

PALACIO

Plaza de Oriente

Encarnación

C. Felipe V

Teatro Real

C. Carlos

Requena Plaza C. Amnistia
Ramales

C. del Factor

San Nicolás

San Nicolás Servitas

Catedral Nuestra Señora de la Almudena

Ermita de la Virgen del Puerto

Po. Ciudad de Plasencia

Cuesta de la Vega

Ayuntamiento Madrid

C. Mayor

Plaza de la V

Puente de Segovia

Parque de Atenas

Calle

C. del Sacramento

Capitanía General

Plaza de la Cruz Verde

Plaza de Cordón

Po. Bajo Virgen del Puerto

C. de Linneo

C. de Manzanares

Juan Duque

Po. de los Melancólicos

Ronda de Segovia

Viaducto

Segovia

Alfonso VI

Bailén

Morería

Plaza Granado

Plaza Beatriz Galindo

Plaza Gabriel Miró

Parque Emir Mohamed I de

Jardines de las Vistillas

C. de Segc

Plaza San Pedro

San Vieja

San Andrés

Plaza San Andrés

2

Centro Estud. Hidrográficos

C. Moreno Nieto

C. Mazarredo

C. San Buenaventura

C. Redondilla

C. de las Aguas

Plaza Humilladero

C. Fósforo

C. Jerte

Carr. San Francisco

C. Don Pedro

3

C. Pizarra

Cuesta Descargas

Basílica San Francisco El Grande

Plaza Francisco San Francisco

Rosario

Gran Vía de San Francisco

C. del Angel

C. Tabernillas

C. Mediodía Grande

C. Humilladero

Avenida del Santo

C. Damiel

C. Ruy González Clavijo

Ronda de Segovia

Ventosa

C. del Aguila

Calatrava

V. de la Paloma

C. San Gato

Paseo Imperial

Cuesta Descargas

C. Bernabé

C. la Paloma

C. Arga

C. Gil Imón

Leonor Vega

Clj. del Mercado

C. Capitán Salazar Martínez

PUERTA DE TOLEDO

Centro Puert

C. Gil

Clj. Particular

IMPERIAL

Glorieta Puerta de Toledo

ℹ

Río Manzanares

Paseo de la Virgen del Puerto

los Melancólicos

C. San Alejandro

Pte. Elevado de S. Isidro

Paseo de los Pontones

Po. de los Pontones

Santa Casilda

de Toledo

Po. de los Olmos

C. San Isidoro

4

Plaza Francisco Morano

Pasillo Verde Ferroviario

Toledo

C. Alejandro

Instituto Nacional Gran Capitán

Duque de Tovar

de los Melancólicos

C. Alejandro

Paseo Imperial

Calle

de las Acacias

C. de Melilla

5

San

Avenida del Manzanares

Estadio Vicente Calderón

C. S. Esteban

Glorieta de las Pirámides

Po.

C. Carmen Cobeña

C. de Melilla

PIRÁMIDES

Paseo

de las

C. Yesera

C. San Pompeyo

Hacienda

Po. de San Illán

Paseo Quince de Ma

C. Pellejeros

González C. Cefer

Av. E. Isar

Puente de Toledo

Avenida

6

Banco de España
Círculo de Bellas Artes
Palacio de Comunicaciones
Plaza de Nicaragua
140
Museo Naval
Museo de Artes Decorativas
Alfonso XII
La Bolsa
C. de Montalbán
C. Alfonso XI
C. de Antonio Maura
Madrazo
Zorrilla
C. de Cubas
Mques. de Cubas
Plaza de la Lealtad
Puerta de España
Po. de la Argentina
Estanque
Museo Thyssen-Bornemisza
Plaza Cánovas del Castillo
Academia Española de la Lengua
Felipe IV
Museo del Ejército
Cason del Buen Retiro
Po. de Parterre
Po. del Paraguay
Plaza de Honduras
C. Méndez Núñez
Puerta Felipe IV
CORTES
Lope de Vega
Museo del Prado
Ruiz de Alarcón
C. del Casado del Alisal
Los Jerónimos
Puerta Murillo
PARQUE DEL
Palaci Cr
C. de las Huertas
Lope de Vega
C. de la Academia
C. Alberto Bosh
Po. San Pablo
a María
Plaza Platería Martínez
C. Moreto
C. Espalter
La Chopera
JERÓNIMOS
de es
C. de Ficar
Plaza de Murillo
Po. del Ecuador
C. Verónica
PASEO DEL PRADO
JARDIN BOTÁNICO
Gobernador
C. Almadén
C. de San Blas
Calle
Puerta del Ángel Caído
Po. del Duque de Fernán Núñez
Viveros Municipales
Gi Áng
Conservatorio de Música
Atocha
C. Claudio Moyano
Ministerio Agricultura, Pesca y Alimentación
Ministerio de Educación y Ciencia
vento anta abel
Santa
C. Hospital
ATOCHA
Plaza Emperador Carlos V
Museo de Etnología
C. Juan Valer
Centro de Arte Reina Sofía
Avenida de la Ciudad
Observatorio Astronómico
Julián
Atocha
Policía
ATOCHA RENFE
de Alfonso XII
Infanta Isabel
Paseo Re
C. Marqués de Valdavia
Calle de Méndez Álvaro
C. Tortosa
de Riego
Rafael
de Murcia
Estación de Atocha
Panteón Hombres Ilustres
Basílica de Atocha
cano
Calle de las Delicias
C. de Te
Nuestra Señora de Las Angustias
PALOS
de las Delicias
C. Pedro Unanue
PALOS DE LA FRONTERA
Palos de la Frontera Calle
de
Ancora
Pje. Ancora
DE MOGUER
Vara de Rey
C. de Canarias
Plaza Luca de Tena
C. de Tarragona
C. de José M. Roquero
C. Garganta Montes
Calle de Méndez Álvaro
Ferrocarril
C. Bustamante
C. Ramírez Prado
C. Bustamante
A
C. del Salado
Ciudad Real
Delicias
ANZUELA
General Palanca
LICIAS
C. de Cáceres
Museo Nacional Ferroviario
Estación de Delicias
144
C. J. de Mariana
C. M. del Campo
C. Ramírez Prado
C. El Atazar
C. Atame

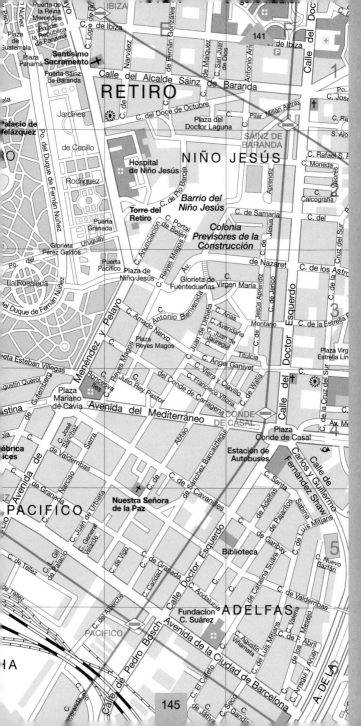

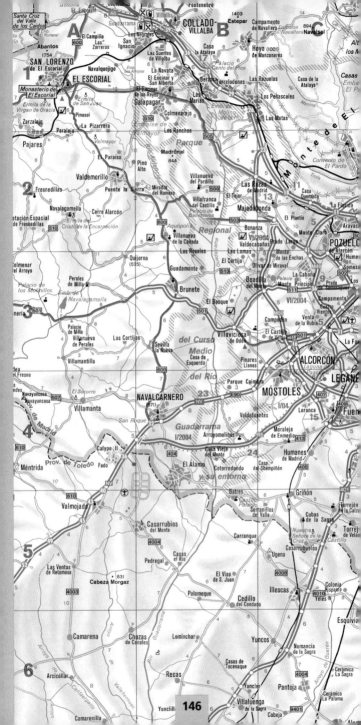

146